stylish
THAI
in minutes

stylish
THAI
in minutes

over 120 inspirational recipes

vatcharin
bhumichitr

Photography by Martin Brigdale
and Somchai Phongphaisarnkit

For David Sweetman

Published in 2006 by SILVERDALE BOOKS
An imprint of Bookmart Ltd, Registered Number 2372865
Trading as Bookmart Limited, Blaby Road, Wigston
Leicester, LE18 4SE

First published in Great Britain in 2004 by
Kyle Cathie Limited

10 9 8 7 6 5 4 3 2 1

ISBN 1 84509 281 3

Vatcharin Bhumichitr is hereby identified as the author of this work in
accordance with Section 77 of the Copyright, Designs and Patents Act 1988.

Text © 2004 Vatcharin Bhumichitr
Food photography © 2004 Martin Brigdale
Travel photography © 2004 Somchai Phongphaisarnkit
Book design © 2004 Kyle Cathie Limited

Senior Editor Muna Reyal
Designer Geoff Hayes
Photographer Martin Brigdale
Home Economist Sunil Vijayakar
Styling Helen Trent
Copy editor Ruth Baldwin
Editorial Assistant Jennifer Wheatley
Production Sha Huxtable and Alice Holloway

A Cataloguing In Publication record for this title is available from the
British Library.

Colour reproduction by Sang Choy
Printed and bound in Singapore by Star Standard

contents

introduction

In Thailand, food and entertainment are inseparable. Eating is always considered to be more fun (*sanuk*) in a group, and the larger the better. We love parties: whether for a young boy about to become a monk, a harvest festival, a wedding, or even a funeral, food and entertainment are always called for and enthusiastically provided. Indeed, the rhythmic sounds of cooking, the chopping of meats, the knives on chopping blocks, the crushing of herbs, the pestle beating in the mortar and the rattle of cooking pans used to be carefully listened to by the single men of the community – a good rhythm being indicative of a good cook and therefore a good wife.

Food and culture

When the Thai food festival was set up ten years ago at London's Battersea Park to promote Thai food, we soon realised that this important ingredient was missing. So I arranged for a stage to be created and invited performers to show the different types of entertainment from Thailand, including Thai classical dance, folk opera (*Likay*) and folk music (*Luk Thoong*). Demonstrations of fruit carving and stalls selling crafts and goods for the home completed the festive atmosphere. The inspiration for this came from the Thai Temple Fair (*Ngarn Wat*) where the local temple holds a festival, normally for a few days, with music, dancing, food, and stands selling all kinds of goods, clothes, toys, household utensils and so on. These festivals are always well attended by local people, who see them as a good opportunity to go out and have a good time, but they also benefit the community by providing money for the local temples, which are still very central to life in Thailand.

In this book I have tried to blend the food and entertainment of Thailand to give you a taste of our culture and to show you how our entertainment, like our cooking, has evolved into a fusion of the old and the new, traditional and stylish. For Thai people, food and entertainment are always enjoyed together, and I have been passionate about them both since I was a child. I would like to share this love with you and so I have begun each chapter with a brief introduction to the various types of entertainment that we enjoy with our food.

I have enjoyed doing the research for this book and hope it will help you to appreciate and understand Thai food and culture.

ingredients

Aubergines

I use several different types of aubergine here. The Thai aubergine most commonly available in Oriental supermarkets is round, pale green and about 2.5cm (1in) in diameter. Do not confuse it with the smaller Thai pea aubergine (generally rarer outside Thailand), which is more bitter.

Beancurd

Beancurd is made from the liquid extracted from yellow soya beans. It is generally available fresh in Oriental supermarkets. The liquid it comes in should be discarded before cooking. Beancurd is delicate and it is best to use it as soon as possible after purchase. It can also be bought, in some places, ready-fried.

Holy Basil

Holy basil is generally available either fresh or dried in Oriental supermarkets. It has a stronger, more intense taste than sweet basil and has to be cooked to release its flavour. If it is not available, sweet basil can be used instead.

Chillies

The chillies I use are generally available from Oriental supermarkets. The smallest are the hottest. The amounts suggested in the recipes will give a taste that Thais would consider okay, but not really hot. You will have to experiment a little to find the level of heat that you like. To reduce the heat use fewer chillies, or deseed them, which will lessen the heat but keep the flavour. Be careful, after cutting or chopping chillies, to wash your hands thoroughly before touching any sensitive areas of your body.

Coconut

Coconut is an essential ingredient in Thai cooking. The coconut palm also produces wood for housing and utensils, leaves for roofing and matting, and gourds for holding food and drink – a useful tree indeed! Fresh coconuts are available at certain times of the year in Oriental supermarkets. The liquid you hear sloshing around inside is coconut juice, not milk, and makes a refreshing drink. Coconut milk and cream are both made from the grated flesh of the coconut, to which warm water is added and the mixture repeatedly squeezed until it becomes cloudy. When this mixture is strained it is coconut milk; if this is left to stand, coconut cream will float to the surface in much the same way as cream does on regular milk. Coconut milk is now widely available in cartons and cans, and even in Thailand many people use canned milk for convenience and speed.

Coriander

Coriander, also known as cilantro or Chinese parsley, is a green herb much used as a garnish in Thai cooking, either whole or chopped. It is generally available in bunches or as a growing herb in a pot from supermarkets and Oriental stores. Coriander root is also much used in Thai cooking, but if you cannot get hold of it, just use an extra length of the lower part of the stalk.

Galangal

This is a type of ginger, with a more translucent, pink tinge. It is peeled, then thinly sliced for ease of cooking. It is generally available in Oriental supermarkets.

Krachai

Another type of ginger, but with thin and relatively straight roots and with a fiercer taste than galangal. It is sometimes available in Oriental stores, but can also be bought dried.

Lemon Grass

Another indispensable ingredient of Thai cuisine. The stalks are bought in bundles of six to eight, and are usually about 20–25cm (8–10in) long. Trim the ends and finely slice the stalks. When bought they do not smell, but when you crush them they give off a refreshing lemon aroma.

Lime Leaves

These are the dark green leaves of the Kaffir lime and impart a pungent lemon-lime flavour. The easiest way to slice them is with kitchen scissors.

Tamarind Water

You can buy the pulp of the tamarind fruit in packets. To extract the juice or water, dissolve the pulp in hot water, then strain the mixture. If tamarind water is not available, use lemon juice, but double the stated quantity.

Stock

Many of the recipes call for stock, and I appreciate that making and keeping stock may not be practicable for many people. In some recipes water can be used instead; in others you will have to use stock cubes. However, if you have the time to make stock, this is how I do it.

For meat stock, simply cover some meat bones with water, bring to the boil and simmer for at least 2 hours, skimming the scum off the surface from time to time. Do not use any herbs or spices. Add more bones as they come along, and remember that you must boil up the stock every day, or freeze it.

For vegetable stock, you will need 1 onion, quartered, 2 carrots, roughly chopped, 2 celery stalks, roughly chopped, 3 or 4 coriander roots and 1 teaspoon black peppercorns. Most hard vegetables will serve, but avoid highly coloured ones such as beetroot. Cover with water and bring to the boil. Continue boiling until the liquid is reduced by about a fifth.

Oil

I do not specify any type of cooking oil, and almost any will do, except olive oil which has too specific a flavour for Thai food.

Sauces

Fish Sauce *Nam Pla*

This is the main flavouring for Thai cooking, for which there is no substitute. It is the salt of South-East Asia. Although it can be made from shrimps, it is most commonly extracted from salted, fermented fish. The best is home-made and has a light whisky colour and a refreshing, salty taste, rather than being dark with a heavy, bitter tang and a powerful, fishy aroma. When buying commercially produced fish sauce I try to find a lighter, rather than darker, liquid. Colour can also indicate if a bottle has been open too long, as the sauce darkens with age. If it has noticeably changed colour, it should be discarded.

Soy Sauce *Siew*

Chinese in origin, soy sauce is made from salted cooked soya beans fermented with flour, after which the liquid is extracted. Commercially there are two varieties on offer: light soy sauce, which is thin, with a clear, delicate flavour, mild enough to be used as a condiment at the table, and dark soy sauce, which is thicker, with a stronger, sweeter flavour, having been fermented with other ingredients such as mushrooms and ginger, that darken the final liquid. The difference between the light and dark is slight, the dark being used to colour food. If you rarely cook Oriental food, a bottle of the light soy sauce will suffice.

Bean Sauce *Tow Jiew*

Bean sauce is made from slightly mashed, fermented soya beans, either black or yellow. It helps to thicken a dish as well as adding flavour. Black bean sauce is thick and deeply coloured, and is used to give a richer flavour than can be achieved with dark soy sauce. Yellow bean sauce is more salty and pungent, but again is a quite subtle refinement. If you rarely cook Oriental food, a jar of black bean sauce will suffice. Nowadays you can buy small jars of both types, which should keep almost indefinitely if refrigerated.

Oyster Sauce *Nam Man Hoy*
This sauce is also of Chinese origin. It is made from oysters which have been cooked in soy sauce and then mixed with seasonings and brine. The result, however, tastes of fish, as might be expected. It should be stored in a refrigerator.

Techniques
With Thai food the time spent actually cooking is quite short, making it ideal for a dinner party, but you do have to have everything prepared beforehand.

Vegetables such as chillies, ginger, shallots, garlic and so on should be finely sliced, or even smashed using the side of a Chinese cleaver. Hard vegetables like carrots and potatoes should be cut into small pieces: green vegetables such as broccoli should be in small florets. Meat should be either minced or sliced into bite-sized pieces.

Nearly every recipe has the instruction 'stir-fry' somewhere in it. As the term implies, the ingredients are stirred while cooking. Simple and fast, stir-frying is best done in a long-handled wok over a high heat. The idea of cooking quickly is to seal in the flavours. Vegetables should be cooked for the minimum amount of time and remain crisp and bright. Do not overcook.

The Thai meal
The ideal Thai meal consists of a number of small dishes shared by a group of friends or family. Rice is ladled onto each plate and everybody takes a little of each dish to eat with the rice – you would never take a large serving – *sharing is essential.* Most of the recipes in this book are suitable for a meal for four people sharing dishes. A typical meal would consist of two or three starters, plus one *yam* (salad) dish brought out before the main meal and served with drinks. Rice would then be served with a soup, a curry and two main dishes, followed by fruit or a dessert. The Thai use spoons and forks, only using chopsticks for noodles.

appetisers
& snacks

classical dance

The Thai dramatic arts, such as the Khon mask dance (pictured right) and the *Lakhon* style of Thai classical dance (pictured on the previous pages), are based on Thai literature.

The *Khon* style of dance performance is characterised by energetic and highly stylised action. The *Khon* dancers begin their training when very young, and will often join Thailand's National Dance and Music College in Bangkok around the age of ten years.

In a *Khon* performance, acting and dancing are inseparable. Each gesture in the play is significant and conveys a meaning. The mood of the moment, such as walking, marching, laughing, is reflected in the pace and character of the background music, which is performed by an orchestra of classical instruments. Singers off-stage perform the narratives and the songs of individual dancers. Usually it is the men who wear the masks on-stage, while the women have high gilded crowns or headdresses.

The *Lakhon* style of dance drama is much less formal than the *Khon* style, and the actors do not normally wear masks, unless in the role of monkeys, or other non-human or celestial beings. *Lakhon* plots are mainly drawn from traditional folk stories such as the *Ramakian*, *Jakatas* and similar folk tales. While *Khon* and *Lakhon* costumes are basically the same, the *Lakhon* dance movements are much more graceful and sensual, with the upper body and hands being used expressively to convey specific emotions.

There are variations of *Lakhon* dance, the main one being *Lakhon Chatri* (the simplest in form and presentation). At *Luk Muang* (Bangkok's City Pillar shrine) you can see the *Lakhon Chatri*, performed at the request of supplicants thanking the deity for wishes granted.

The more stylised and graceful *Lakhon Nai* dance was primarily seen among the court ladies at the palace. Men, however, monopolised the *Lakhon Nok* plays, seen outside the palace and consisting of lively music, humour and rapid animated movements.

Traditional Thai dance is embedded in the ancient culture of my beautiful land. Of course these days Thai youths are as influenced as all others around the world by the modern trends in popular music, but it is my hope that enough of each new generation will want to invest their time, energy and commitment to continuing the traditional dance culture to preserve this ancient heritage for all to enjoy.

I have chosen classical dance to open this chapter, as the presentation of appetisers and snacks is often as elaborate as the staging of these performances. I hope that you will be tempted to try the recipes, and if in Thailand, go and see some dance.

spring rolls
po pia tod

1 tablespoon cornflour, mixed with a little water to make a paste
6 large spring roll sheets, quartered
Oil, for deep-frying

For the filling
110g (4oz) soaked wun sen noodles, finely chopped
50g (2oz) pre-soaked dried black fungus mushrooms, finely chopped
50g (2oz) beansprouts
50g (2oz) carrots, finely diced
1 teaspoon finely chopped garlic
1 teaspoon light soy sauce
1/2 teaspoon ground white pepper

For the sweet chilli sauce
6 tablespoons rice vinegar
4 tablespoons sugar
1/2 teaspoon salt
3 small fresh red or green chillies, finely chopped

Place all the filling ingredients in a mixing bowl and stir well. Set aside. Heat the vinegar and stir in the sugar until dissolved. Stir in the salt and chillies. Turn into a bowl and set aside. Stir just before serving.

Place a little filling on each quartered spring roll sheet. Fold in two opposite corners, then roll across them to form a plump roll. Use a little of the cornflour paste to seal. Heat the oil and deep-fry the rolls until golden brown, drain on kitchen paper and serve with the sweet chilli sauce and salad leaves such as lettuce, mint leaves and cucumber.

Preparation time: 15 minutes   Cooking time: 5 minutes

prawn and lychee spring rolls
po pia kung

12 spring roll sheets, each 10cm (4in) square
6 large raw prawns, peeled but with the tail left on, de-veined and
  cut in half lengthways
6 large lychees (fresh or tinned), peeled and roughly chopped
Salt and ground black pepper
1 egg, beaten
Oil, for deep-frying
Sweet chilli sauce (see recipe, left), to serve

Take one spring roll sheet and fold over one corner towards the centre. Lay a prawn half on the sheet, with its tail hanging over the folded edge. Lay half of one chopped lychee along the length of the prawn and sprinkle with salt and pepper. Roll up the sheet over the prawn, so that you are left with a cylinder with the tail protruding from one end. Seal the spring roll with beaten egg. Repeat the process to make the remaining spring rolls. Set aside.

Heat a pan of oil for deep-frying to 200°C (400°F). Deep-fry the spring rolls until they are golden brown all over. Drain on kitchen paper and serve hot with the sweet chilli sauce.

Preparation time: 10 minutes   Cooking time: 5 minutes

steamed stuffed won ton

kanom jeep

2 eggs

15 whole black peppercorns

2 coriander roots, roughly chopped

2 tablespoons oil

2 small garlic cloves, finely chopped

110g (4oz) bamboo shoots, finely diced

110g (4oz) water chestnuts, finely diced

1 large onion, finely diced

2 teaspoons plain flour

2 tablespoons light soy sauce

1 teaspoon sugar

20 sheets won ton pastry

Lettuce and coriander leaves, to garnish

For the sour soy sauce

3 tablespoons light soy sauce

1 tablespoon white vinegar

1 teaspoon sugar

3 small fresh red or green chillies, finely chopped

Hard-boil the eggs, chop finely and set aside.

In a mortar, pound the peppercorns and coriander roots until a paste forms, then set aside.

In a wok or frying pan, heat the oil, fry the garlic until golden brown and set aside with the oil.

In a bowl, mix the bamboo shoots, water chestnuts, onion, the pepper and coriander root paste, flour, soy sauce, sugar and chopped eggs, stirring well until a firm mixture is formed.

Separate the won ton sheets. At the centre of each, place a nugget of filling. Gather up the edges of the pastry square and crimp together to form a tiny cup. Arrange the cups in a steamer and steam for 15 minutes.

Meanwhile, make the sour soy sauce by stirring all the ingredients together in a small bowl.

Just before serving, drip a little of the reserved garlic oil on to each won ton cup, garnish with the lettuce and coriander leaves and serve with the sour soy sauce.

Preparation time: 15 minutes   Cooking time: 15 minutes

vegetable won ton geo tod

20 sheets won ton pastry
Oil, for deep-frying, plus 1 tablespoon

For the filling
2 teaspoons garlic, roughly chopped
1 teaspoon whole black peppercorns
Oil, for deep-frying
75g (3oz) potato, finely diced
75g (3oz) onion, finely diced
75g (3oz) carrots, finely diced
75g (3oz) boiled sweetcorn (off the cob)
1/2 teaspoon salt
1 tablespoon curry powder
1 tablespoon light soy sauce
1 teaspoon sugar
Sweet chilli sauce (see page 17)

To make the filling, pound together the garlic and peppercorns in a mortar to form a paste. Heat 1 tablespoon of oil, briefly fry the paste, then add the other filling ingredients in succession, stirring constantly. Set aside.

Place a nugget of the filling at the centre of each won ton pastry square. Fold the square in half diagonally to make a triangle. Use a little water to seal the sides. Deep-fry the stuffed won ton until golden brown, drain on kitchen paper and serve with the sweet chilli sauce.

Preparation time: 10 minutes   Cooking time: 5 minutes

fried sweet potato mantod

Food stalls in Thailand sell bananas and taro cooked in this way. (Taro is a tuber that is sometimes mixed with flavouring and served as a dessert).

1 egg
3 tablespoons coconut milk
2 tablespoons plain flour
1 tablespoon sugar
1/2 teaspoon salt
1 tablespoon sesame seeds
275g (10oz) sweet potato, peeled and cut into large chips
Oil, for deep-frying

In a large bowl, combine the egg, coconut milk, flour, sugar, salt and sesame seeds and mix well. Add the sweet potato chips and stir until they are well coated.

Heat the oil and deep-fry the battered chips until golden brown. Drain well before serving.

Preparation time: 5 minutes   Cooking time: 5 minutes

deep-fried yellow bean paste baa yir

For the paste
110g (4oz) dried moong beans, soaked in water for 30 minutes and drained
1 tablespoon plain flour
2 teaspoons red curry paste
1 tablespoon light soy sauce
1 teaspoon sugar
2 Kaffir lime leaves, rolled into a thin cylinder and finely sliced into slivers
Oil, for deep-frying

For the sweet sauce
4 tablespoons sugar
6 tablespoons rice vinegar
1/2 teaspoon salt

To make the sauce, gently heat the three ingredients until the sugar dissolves. Allow to cool before serving.

In a mortar, pound the drained moong beans to form a paste. Add the other ingredients in succession, stirring well. Pluck a small piece of the paste and form into a ball the size of a walnut. Do not mould· too tightly. Deep-fry the balls in hot oil until golden brown, drain and serve with the thick sweet sauce.

Preparation time: 5 minutes   Cooking time: 5 minutes

steamed mussels with galangal
hoy ob ka

This is the Thai version of steamed mussels and we consider it tastier than the European versions. I hope you do too!

450g (1lb) mussels
50g (2oz) galangal, sliced lengthways into matchsticks
6 Kaffir lime leaves, roughly chopped

For the sauce
2 tablespoons sugar
4 small fresh red chillies, lightly crushed
3 tablespoons fish sauce
3 tablespoons lemon juice

Scrub the mussels thoroughly under cold running water, scraping off any barnacles or beards. Put the mussels in a heavy-based pan on a high heat. Throw in the galangal and Kaffir lime leaves, stirring thoroughly, then cover the pan. Leave for a moment, then lift and shake the pan to toss the mussels and mix the ingredients. Repeat this process for 5–8 minutes, or until the shells have opened. Discard any mussels that have not opened.

To make the sauce, mix all the ingredients in a bowl and set aside.

Ladle the cooked mussels on to a serving dish and serve with the sauce. You can eat the galangal, taking a little with each mussel.

Preparation time: 10 minutes   Cooking time: 8 minutes

oysters with spicy dressing
hoy nang lom manow

6 oysters
Crushed ice
Coriander leaves, to garnish

For the dressing
3 tablespoons lime juice
1 teaspoon sugar
2 garlic cloves, finely chopped
2 fresh red or green chillies, finely chopped
Salt, to taste

Shuck the oysters, removing them from the shells into a bowl. Rinse the shells thoroughly and dry them.

To make the dressing, place all the ingredients in a bowl, mix thoroughly and leave to one side.

Arrange the oysters with their shells on the crushed ice, spoon over the dressing, then garnish with coriander leaves and serve.

Preparation time: 10 minutes   Cooking time: 0 minutes

deep-fried prawn and sweetcorn cakes
tod man kung

20 whole black peppercorns

3 garlic cloves

1/2 teaspoon salt

1 large dried red chilli, finely chopped

Fresh sweetcorn kernels from 3 uncooked cobs

225g (8oz) raw prawns (peeled weight), chopped

1 tablespoon fish sauce

1 teaspoon sugar

Oil, for deep-frying

Plum sauce (see page 25), to serve

In a mortar, pound together the peppercorns, garlic, salt and dried chilli to form a paste. Add the sweetcorn and pound well into the paste. Add the raw prawns, fish sauce and sugar and pound well.

You should now have a thick paste, which you mould into about ten round patties approximately 5cm (2in) in diameter. Deep-fry the patties in batches in hot oil until golden brown, then drain. Serve hot with plum sauce.

Preparation time: 8 minutes   Cooking time: 5 minutes

sweetcorn cakes
tod man khao pod

225g (8oz) sweetcorn kernels (tinned or frozen; if tinned, drain well)

1 tablespoon curry powder

2 tablespoons rice flour

3 tablespoons wheat flour

1/2 teaspoon salt

2 tablespoons light soy sauce

Oil, for deep-frying

For the sauce

4 tablespoons rice vinegar

2 tablespoons sugar

2.5cm (1in) piece of cucumber, quartered lengthways, then finely sliced

2 shallots, finely sliced

1 tablespoon ground roasted peanuts

1 small fresh red or green chilli, finely sliced

To make the sauce, heat the vinegar and sugar together in a small pan, stirring constantly, until the sugar dissolves and the mixture begins to thicken slightly. Remove from the heat and allow to cool. Pour into a bowl, add the remaining ingredients and stir thoroughly. Set aside.

In a bowl, mix together the sweetcorn, curry powder, flours, salt and soy sauce. Heat the oil until a light haze appears. Take a tablespoon of the mixture and shape into a small cake, then slide into the hot oil. Fry until golden brown. Continue until you have used all the mixture. Remove cakes from the oil and drain. Serve hot with the sauce.

Preparation time: 8 minutes   Cooking time: 5 minutes

crab and coconut cakes with plum sauce

tod man poo

225g (8oz) fresh crab meat

25g (1oz) unsweetened desiccated coconut

1 egg

2 garlic cloves, finely chopped

1 tablespoon fish sauce

1 tablespoon oyster sauce

Pinch of ground white pepper

Fine dried white breadcrumbs, for coating

Oil, for deep-frying

For the plum sauce

1 preserved plum

6 tablespoons rice vinegar

4 tablespoons sugar

2 small fresh red or green chillies, finely chopped

First make the sauce. Use a fork to scrape the plum flesh from the stone. Heat the vinegar and add the sugar and plum flesh, stirring until the sugar dissolves. Simmer until a thin syrup begins to form, then remove from the heat. Stir in the chillies, pour into a bowl and set aside.

In a mixing bowl, stir together the crab, coconut, egg, garlic, sauces and pepper. Knead with your fingers, then form into small patties. Roll in the breadcrumbs until well coated.

Heat a pan of oil to 200°C (400°F). Deep-fry the patties until golden brown. Drain on kitchen paper and serve with the plum sauce.

Preparation time: 10 minutes   Cooking time: 5 minutes

deep-fried spare ribs with chilli and lemon grass
gra dook moo tod

If you are fortunate enough to have a barbecue, you can use that instead of deep-frying them.

2 tablespoons sesame oil
2 garlic cloves, finely chopped and crushed
1 lemon grass stalk, finely chopped and pounded
4 small fresh red chillies, finely chopped and pounded
1/2 teaspoon salt
1 teaspoon sugar
2 tablespoons fish sauce
450g (1lb) young pork spare ribs, chopped into 5cm (2in) pieces
  (ask your butcher to prepare them)
Oil for deep-frying
For the lime dip
1/2 teaspoon salt
1 teaspoon ground white pepper
4 tablespoons lime juice

Mix the sesame oil, garlic, lemon grass, chillies, salt, sugar and fish sauce. Add the spare rib pieces, mix and leave to marinate for at least 1 hour.

Heat the oil and deep-fry the spare ribs, in batches, until golden brown. Remove from the oil, drain and keep warm until they are all done.

While the spare ribs are frying, make the lime dip. Mix all the ingredients together and pour in a dipping bowl. Place the spare ribs on a plate and serve with the dip.

Preparation time: 10 minutes   Cooking time: 5 minutes

grilled spicy sliced steak
nua nam tok

The Thai name for this dish translates as 'beef waterfall'. This is because when you eat it in Thailand you perspire so much you look like a waterfall! If you don't like it too hot, reduce the chilli powder.

225g (8oz) lean beef steak
4 tablespoons beef stock
2 tablespoons fish sauce
3 tablespoons lemon juice
1 teaspoon chilli powder
1 teaspoon sugar
2 shallots or 1 onion, finely sliced
1 tablespoon ground brown rice
Lettuce, cucumber, radish and coriander leaves, to garnish

Arrange the lettuce, cucumber, radish and coriander leaves on a serving plate.

Preheat the grill and when it is hot, grill the steak quickly – the meat should be rare in the middle. Slice it thinly and set aside.

Put the stock, fish sauce, lemon juice, chilli powder and sugar in a small pan over a high heat. Stir quickly and bring to the boil. Add the steak slices and stir; add the shallots or onion and stir, then add the ground rice and stir once to mix. Cook for a second, then turn the mixture on to the prepared plate and serve.

Preparation time: 5 minutes   Cooking time: 8 minutes

steamed spare ribs with black bean

gra dook moo nueng dow jeow

900g (2lb) small pork spare ribs, chopped into 2.5cm (1in) pieces
  (ask your butcher to prepare them)
1 teaspoon salt
1 tablespoon sugar
2 teaspoons black bean sauce
2 garlic cloves, finely chopped
2 teaspoons cornflour
2 long fresh chillies (1 red and 1 green), finely sliced

In a large bowl, mix the rib pieces with the rest of the ingredients, making sure each piece is coated with the mixture. Divide the mixture between four to six small serving bowls.

Using your largest steamer (or largest pan containing enough upturned bowls to support all the bowls of ribs), steam the ribs in the bowls for 20–25 minutes and serve.

Preparation time: 5 minutes   Cooking time: 25 minutes

spicy prawns
pla gung

This can be made with any combination of seafood.

2 tablespoons vegetable stock

2 tablespoons fish sauce

1/2 teaspoon chilli powder

6 large raw prawns, peeled and de-veined

1 lemon grass stalk, finely chopped

3 shallots, coarsely chopped

4 Kaffir lime leaves, finely sliced

1 teaspoon sugar

2 tablespoons lemon juice

2 spring onions, finely chopped

Boil the stock, fish sauce and chilli powder in a small pan. Add the prawns and cook quickly until they are opaque.

Add the remaining ingredients, stir well, remove from the heat and transfer to a serving plate.

Preparation time: 5 minutes   Cooking time: 3 minutes

fried prawns with
sesame seeds
kung chup bang tod

The Chinese eat sesame seeds because apart from being tasty, they help to make your hair black and shiny. The batter and dipping sauce can also be used for vegetables: carrots, beans, celery, courgettes and so on.

Oil, for deep-frying

12 large raw prawns, deheaded, peeled, tail left on, and de-veined

For the batter

150g (5oz) plain flour

1/2 teaspoon salt

1 egg

1 tablespoon sesame seeds

For the dipping sauce

3 tablespoons light soy sauce

1/2 teaspoon sugar

5–6 coriander leaves, coarsely chopped

In a bowl, mix the flour and salt. Break the egg into the mixture and mix thoroughly. Add 225ml(8fl oz) water and sesame seeds gradually, whisking constantly. You should have a thick, creamy batter.

Heat the oil until a light haze appears. Dip each prawn into the batter, ensuring it is well coated, and drop into the hot oil. Deep-fry until golden brown. Remove from the oil, drain and place on a serving dish.

To make the dipping sauce, mix the soy sauce with the sugar and chopped coriander leaves in a small bowl. Serve with the prawns.

Preparation time: 5 minutes   Cooking time: 3 minutes

barbecued prawns on lemon grass
kung hoh takrai

600g (1¹/4lb) medium raw prawns, peeled and de-veined
4 garlic cloves, crushed
4 spring onions, chopped
2 teaspoons sugar
2 teaspoons fish sauce
2 teaspoons cornflour
1 bacon rasher, finely chopped
10 fresh lemon grass stalks, each about 14cm (5¹/2in) long
Plum sauce (see page 25), to serve

Put the prawns, garlic, spring onions, sugar, fish sauce, cornflour and bacon in a food processor and process until fine and pasty. With lightly oiled hands, mould level tablespoons of the prawn mixture around the centre of each lemon grass stalk.

Heat a greased barbecue hotplate, griddle pan or grill until hot and cook the stalks until the prawn mixture is cooked through, turning occasionally during cooking. Serve with the plum sauce.

Preparation time: 5 minutes   Cooking time: 8 minutes

prawns wrapped in noodles
gung sarong

1 egg
¹/2 teaspoon salt
¹/2 teaspoon sugar
¹/2 teaspoon ground white pepper
6 raw king prawns, peeled and de-veined
1 nest of ba mee noodles
Oil, for deep-frying
Sweet chilli sauce (see page 17) or plum sauce (see page 25), to serve

In a bowl, mix the egg, salt, sugar and pepper together. Add the prawns and mix well. Lift three or four strands of noodle and wrap them round each prawn, winding the strands into a mesh that thickly covers the prawn.

Heat the oil until a light haze appears and deep-fry the wrapped prawns until golden brown. Drain and serve with the sweet chilli sauce or the plum sauce.

Preparation time: 10 minutes   Cooking time: 3 minutes

hot-and-sour crispy squid and lime salad
yam pla muk grob

1 small lime

Oil, for deep-frying

200g (7oz) cleaned baby squid, sliced into rings

30 sweet basil leaves

2 lemon grass stalks, trimmed of all tough leaves and finely chopped
  into rings

10 Kaffir lime leaves, rolled into a thin cylinder and finely sliced
  across

110g (4oz) roasted peanuts

5 small fresh red or green chillies, finely chopped

½ teaspoon salt

Cut the lime into quarters. Remove and discard the core and most of the pips. Dice the segments, with the skin, to make tiny cubes, removing any remaining pips. Set aside.

Heat a pan of oil for deep-frying to 200°C (400°F). Using a mesh sieve or strainer, deep-fry the squid until golden and crispy. Drain on kitchen paper and turn into a large mixing bowl. Deep-fry the basil until crispy; drain and turn into the bowl. Repeat the process with the lemon grass and then the Kaffir lime leaves.

Add all the remaining ingredients, including the reserved lime cubes, to the bowl. Mix well, then turn on to a plate and serve.

Preparation time: 8 minutes   Cooking time: 10 minutes

crispy rice with pork, prawn and coconut sauce
khao tang naa tang

2 garlic cloves, roughly chopped

1 teaspoon chopped coriander root

1 teaspoon whole black peppercorns

110g (4oz) minced pork

50g (2oz) minced raw prawns

2 tablespoons oil

2 shallots, finely chopped

225 ml (8fl oz) coconut milk

1 tablespoon fish sauce

1 tablespoon light soy sauce

1 tablespoon tamarind water

1 teaspoon sugar

2 tablespoons ground roasted peanuts

1 large fresh red chilli, sliced lengthways

Fresh coriander leaves, to garnish

Crispy rice (see page 107), to serve

In a mortar, pound the garlic, coriander root and peppercorns together to form a paste. In a bowl, mix the minced pork and prawns together. In a large pan, heat the oil and stir in the garlic paste. Add the mixed pork and prawns and stir well. Stirring constantly, add each of the remaining ingredients in succession (apart from the garnish).

Turn on to a plate, garnish with chilli and coriander leaves and serve with the crispy rice.

Preparation time: 10 minutes   Cooking time: 10 minutes

steamed scallops with garlic

hoy nung kratiem jeow

A delicate starter, easy to make but very luxurious.

6 scallops on the shell, cleaned

3 tablespoons oil

3 garlic cloves, finely chopped

2 small fresh red or green chillies, sliced into fine rings

For the sauce

3 tablespoons light soy sauce

2.5cm (1in) piece fresh ginger, finely chopped

1 teaspoon sugar

1 small red chilli, finely chopped

For the garnish

2 tablespoons spring onion, finely sliced

6 coriander leaves

Set the scallops on their shells in a steamer over 2.5–5cm (1–2in) hot water. In a small frying pan, heat the oil, add the garlic and fry until golden brown. Pour a spoonful of garlic and oil over each scallop, add a little sliced chilli, cover, and steam over medium heat for 10–15 minutes until the scallops are cooked.

While the scallops steam, mix together all the sauce ingredients in a small bowl.

When the scallops are cooked, remove from the steamer, place on a serving dish and garnish with the spring onion and coriander leaves. Serve the sauce on the side.

Preparation time: 5 minutes   Cooking time: 15 minutes

skewered marinated pork   moo ping

This dish can be prepared with chicken if you wish. It makes about 12 skewers.

2 garlic cloves, finely chopped
6 coriander roots, finely chopped
4 tablespoons fish sauce
1 tablespoon light soy sauce
110ml (4fl oz) thick coconut cream
110ml (4fl oz) oil
1 tablespoon sugar
½ teaspoon ground white pepper
450g (1lb) lean pork, thinly sliced into 4 x 7.5cm (1½ x 3in) pieces
Lettuce, parsley or coriander leaves, to garnish

For the sauce
1 tablespoon fish sauce
2 tablespoons lemon juice
1 tablespoon light soy sauce
1 teaspoon chilli powder
1 tablespoon sugar
1 tablespoon coriander leaves, coarsely chopped

Combine all the skewer ingredients, except the pork and the garnish, until they are thoroughly blended. Add the pork and mix in, making sure that each piece is well coated. Let stand for at least 30 minutes; longer if possible.

While the meat is marinating, place all the sauce ingredients in a small bowl and mix well. Taste; if too hot, add more fish sauce, lemon juice and sugar.

Preheat the grill to high. Take twelve 15–20cm (6–8in) wooden skewers and thread two pieces of meat on each, making sure that as much of the surface of the meat as possible will be exposed to the grill. (Make more skewers if you have meat left over.)

Grill under a high heat for 2–3 minutes each side, or until the meat is completely cooked through. Serve on a dish garnished with lettuce, parsley or coriander, with the sauce on the side.

Marinating time: 30 minutes   Cooking time: 5 minutes

pork with fruit and peanuts
ma ho

This dish is an interesting contrast in both colour and texture between the fruit (which can be pineapple instead of tangerines if you prefer) and meat mixture, topped with chillies and coriander.

2 tangerines, peeled and separated into segments
1 tablespoon oil
2 garlic cloves, finely chopped
2 shallots, finely chopped
75g (3oz) minced pork
1 tablespoon fish sauce
1 teaspoon sugar
2 tablespoons coarsely pounded roasted peanuts
½ teaspoon ground black pepper

For the garnish
2 fresh red chillies, deseeded and cut into slivers
Coriander leaves

Lay the tangerine segments on a dish. In a frying pan, heat the oil and fry the garlic and shallots until light brown. Add the pork, fish sauce and sugar and stir-fry until the pork is cooked through. Stir in the peanuts and ground pepper and mix thoroughly. Remove from the heat.

Place a heaped teaspoon of the meat mixture on each tangerine segment. Garnish with red chillies and coriander leaves.

Preparation time: 5 minutes   Cooking time: 5 minutes

chicken wings with lemon grass
gai ta krai

This is good with sticky rice, and perfect when travelling as it can be eaten cold.

3 lemon grass stalks, finely chopped
2 small fresh red chillies, finely chopped
450g (1lb) chicken wings
3 tablespoons oyster sauce
1 tablespoon fish sauce
1 teaspoon sugar
Oil, for deep-frying
Sweet chilli sauce (see page 17), to serve

In a large bowl, mix all the ingredients together. Leave to marinate for 15 minutes. Heat the oil and deep-fry the chicken wings until golden brown. Drain and serve with the sweet chilli sauce.

Marinating time: 15 minutes   Cooking time: 5 minutes

heavenly beef
nua sawan

In Thailand, after marinating the meat we leave it in the sun to dry for a day.

4 tablespoons fish sauce
1 tablespoon palm sugar
2 teaspoons roughly pounded coriander seeds
450g (1lb) lean tender beef steak, thinly sliced
Oil, for deep-frying

In a saucepan, heat the fish sauce, then add the palm sugar and stir well until it has dissolved. Stir in the coriander seeds, mix well, then remove from the heat and leave to cool.

Place the beef slices in a bowl, add the fish sauce mixture and mix well. Leave to marinate for at least 1 hour. Remove the meat and leave to drain overnight on a rack set over a large plate.

Heat the oil and deep-fry the dried meat until it is dark brown. Drain on kitchen paper and serve.

Marinating time: 1 hour   Cooking time: 5 minutes

fried beef balls
tord man nua

175g (6oz) minced beef
3 garlic cloves, chopped
1 small onion, finely chopped
1/2 teaspoon ground black pepper
1 tablespoon fish sauce
1 tablespoon light soy sauce
1/2 teaspoon sugar
1 egg
2 tablespoons finely chopped coriander leaves
Plain flour, for coating
Oil, for deep-frying
Sweet chilli sauce (see page 17), to serve

In a bowl, mix together the minced beef, garlic, onion, pepper, fish sauce, soy sauce, sugar, egg and coriander leaves until well blended. Form into firm balls 2.5cm (1in) in diameter and lightly dust the balls with flour.

Heat the oil in a wok until a haze appears and deep-fry the balls until golden brown. Drain on kitchen paper and serve with chilli sauce.

Preparation time: 3 minutes   Cooking time: 5 minutes

chicken satay

satay

1 teaspoon coriander seeds

1 teaspoon cumin seeds

3 skinless chicken breasts

2 tablespoons light soy sauce

1 teaspoon salt

4 tablespoons oil

1 tablespoon curry powder

1 tablespoon ground turmeric

8 tablespoons coconut milk

3 tablespoons sugar

For the peanut sauce

2 tablespoons oil

3 garlic cloves, finely chopped

1 tablespoon dry curry paste (see page 73)

8 tablespoons coconut milk

225ml (8fl oz) chicken stock

1 tablespoon sugar

1 teaspoon salt

1 tablespoon lemon juice

4 tablespoons crushed roasted peanuts

Roast the coriander and cumin seeds gently in a small frying pan without oil for about 5 minutes, stirring and shaking to ensure they do not burn. Remove from the heat and grind together to make a fine powder. (You could use ready-ground seeds if more convenient.)

With a sharp knife, cut the chicken breasts into fine slices 7.5cm x 4cm x 5mm (3in x $1^1/_2$in x $^1/_4$in). Put the slices in a bowl and add all the remaining ingredients, including the ground coriander and cumin seeds. Mix thoroughly and leave to marinate overnight, or for 8 hours (you can prepare in the morning for the evening meal).

To make the peanut sauce, heat the oil in a frying pan until a light haze appears. Add the chopped garlic and fry until golden brown. Add the curry paste, mix well and cook for a few more seconds. Add the coconut milk, mix in well and cook for a few seconds. Add the stock, sugar, salt and lemon juice and stir to blend. Cook for a minute or two, stirring constantly. Add the crushed peanuts, stir well, then pour the sauce into a bowl.

When you are ready to cook the chicken, preheat the grill (Thais would normally use a charcoal or barbecue grill). Using 18–20cm (7–8in) wooden satay sticks, thread two pieces of the marinated chicken on each stick – not straight through the meat, but rather as if you were gathering or smocking a piece of material. Grill the satays for about 6–8 minutes until the meat is cooked through, turning to ensure they are browned on both sides. Serve with the peanut sauce.

Marinating time: 8 hours   Cooking time: 8 minutes

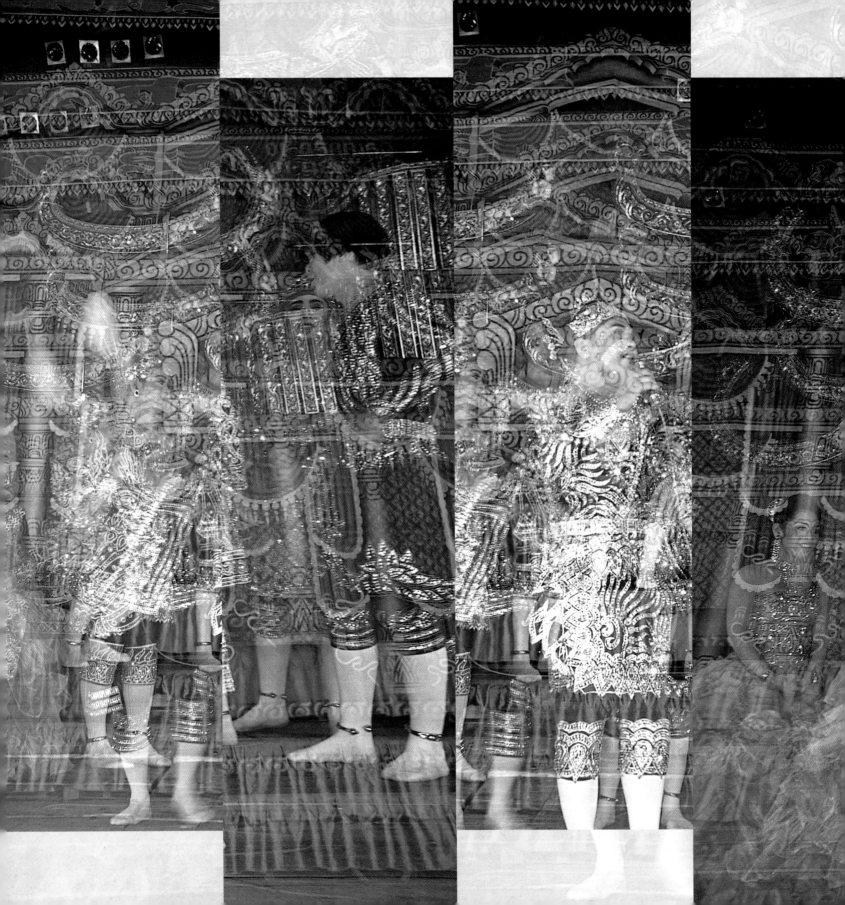

salads & soups

theatre

Likay is a type of folk theatre enjoyed by many people and is especially popular in the provinces, where it is still an important feature of many festivals. It is a burlesque form of the more sedate *Lakhon* (see page 14) and contains elements of pantomime, comic folk opera and social satire (pictured right and on previous pages). This kind of entertainment is generally performed against a simple painted backdrop at Temple Fairs.

The stories are usually derived from much-loved court dramas, but have been embellished with local references and anecdotes. The dialogue is spontaneous, spiced with outrageous puns and double entendre. Each performance is accompanied by traditional music and dance, which some troupes like to exaggerate in a rather camp fashion. The costumes and make-up are often dramatic – Thai people talk of 'dressing up like *Likay*' if they want to describe exaggerated clothing and make-up.

Likay theatre is often an inspired combination of sources and styles, mixing words and music, costume and make-up to create something unique for each performance. The ingredients here are similarly thrown together, though in a more considered fashion, to give you flavoursome salads and subtly balanced soups.

bamboo shoot salad

yam normai

This dish originates from Isaan, in the north-east of Thailand, and would be eaten there with sticky rice.

110g (4oz) bamboo shoots
2 shallots, peeled
1 garlic clove, peeled
4 tablespoons vegetable stock
2 tablespoons lemon juice
2 tablespoons light soy sauce
1 teaspoon sugar
1 teaspoon chilli powder
2 teaspoons dry-fried sesame seeds
10 mint leaves
1 spring onion, finely chopped
2 large Chinese cabbage leaves
2 long beans, chopped into 10cm (4in) lengths (French beans may be substituted)

With a knife, scrape the pieces of bamboo shoot to make long matchstick gratings and set aside.

Grill the shallots and garlic until they are soft and give off a pleasant, slightly burnt aroma without actually burning. Place in a mortar and pound together, then set aside.

Put the stock into a saucepan and bring to the boil. Add the bamboo shoot gratings, the pounded shallot and garlic, lemon juice, soy sauce, sugar and chilli powder and stir well. Remove from the heat. Add the sesame seeds, mint leaves and spring onion, stirring briefly. Arrange the Chinese cabbage leaves and the long beans around the edge of a serving dish, turn the mixture into the centre and serve.

Preparation time: 3 minutes   Cooking time: 5 minutes

green papaya salad
som tam

Som Tam is now as well known as *Tom Yam* and *Pad Thai*. If prepared with soy sauce this is suitable for vegetarians.

110g (4oz) green papaya, peeled and seeds removed
1 garlic clove
3 small fresh red or green chillies
1 tablespoon roasted peanuts
25g (1oz) long beans, chopped into 2.5cm (1in) lengths
  (French beans may be substituted)
2 tablespoons lemon juice
3 tablespoons light soy sauce or fish sauce
1 teaspoon sugar
1 medium tomato, chopped into segments
2 large leaves Chinese cabbage

Finely shred the papaya flesh with a cheese grater or chop it very finely into long, thin shreds. Set aside.

In a mortar, lightly pound the garlic, add the chillies, and lightly pound again. Add the peanuts and lightly pound while occasionally stirring with a spoon to prevent the resulting paste from thickening. Add the long beans and slightly bruise them. Add the shredded papaya, lightly pound and stir until all the ingredients are blended together. Add the lemon juice, soy or fish sauce and sugar and stir into the mixture. Finally add the tomato, stirring once.

Put the cabbage leaves on a plate and turn the mixture on to them.

Preparation time: 10 minutes   Cooking time: 0 minutes

mango yam with cashew nuts
yam mamuang

The difficulty with this dish is to find unripe green mangoes; otherwise it is delightfully easy to make. Use green cooking apples if you can't get hold of the mangoes.

1 small green mango, peeled and grated or finely chopped
3 small fresh red or green chillies, finely chopped
3 shallots, finely chopped
1 teaspoon sugar
1 garlic clove, finely chopped
2 tablespoons lemon juice
1/2 teaspoon salt
2 tablespoons whole roasted cashews

Briefly soak the grated or chopped mango in cold water to remove any syrup. Drain and put in a large bowl with all the other ingredients. Stir well and serve.

Preparation time: 3 minutes   Cooking time: 0 minutes

salad of black fungus mushrooms

yam het hoo noo

When I was young, my mother used to make jellyfish salad, which I loved. When I came to live in Europe, it was impossible to find jellyfish, so I substituted mushrooms, as the texture is similar.

1 garlic clove

3 small fresh red or green chillies

1 teaspoon sugar

2 tablespoons lemon juice

2 tablespoons light soy sauce

50g (2oz) pre-soaked dried black fungus mushrooms, cut into strips

50g (2oz) celery, chopped lengthways into 2.5cm (1in) matchsticks

25g (1oz) carrot, chopped lengthways into 2.5cm (1in) matchsticks

25g (1oz) cucumber, chopped lengthways into 2.5cm (1in) matchsticks

2 spring onions, chopped lengthways into 2.5cm (1in) matchsticks

1 tablespoon crushed roasted peanuts

1 teaspoon dry-fried sesame seeds

1 shallot, finely chopped into rings

4–5 lettuce leaves

Coriander leaves, to garnish

In a mortar, pound the garlic and chillies until well crushed. Combine with the sugar, lemon juice and soy to make a sauce.

Place the mushrooms, celery, carrot, cucumber and spring onions in a bowl. Pour over the sauce and stir well. Add the peanuts, sesame seeds and shallot rings and stir. Arrange the lettuce leaves on a serving dish and place the mixture on them. Garnish with coriander leaves.

Preparation time: 10 minutes   Cooking time: 0 minutes

vegetable salad with peanut sauce

salad kaek

For the sauce

2 tablespoons oil

1 tablespoon red curry paste

450ml (16fl oz) coconut milk

½ teaspoon salt

1 tablespoon sugar

1 teaspoon tamarind water

4 tablespoons crushed roasted peanuts

First make the sauce. Heat the oil in a wok or large frying pan, and stir in the curry paste. Add the coconut milk and stir well. Add all the remaining ingredients together, continuing to stir. Cook briefly until the coconut milk comes to the boil. Remove at once from the heat.

To make the salad, heat the oil and deep-fry the beancurd until golden. Remove, drain and set aside.

Arrange all the vegetables in a salad bowl. Shell and quarter the eggs, then place them in the bowl. Thinly slice the beancurd and add to the bowl.

Serve the salad with the sauce, either separately or poured over the salad and tossed.

Preparation time: 10 minutes   Cooking time: 15 minutes

This dish originates from the Muslim area in the south of Thailand and is vegetarian.

Oil, for deep-frying

2 blocks of beancurd, about 5cm (2in) square

110g (4oz) beansprouts

110g (4oz) long beans, chopped into 2.5cm (1in) lengths

1 medium tomato, thinly sliced

110g (4oz) cucumber, thinly sliced

110g (4oz) white cabbage, thinly sliced, then broken up into strands

2 hard-boiled eggs

chicken salad with mint and nuts

yam gai

This recipe is one of my grandmother's recipes, and I have changed it little over the years.

175g (6oz) skinless chicken breast fillet

75g (3oz) beansprouts

75g (3oz) cucumber, cut in half lengthways, deseeded, then cut into
 5cm (2in) matchsticks

75g (3oz) onion, finely chopped

2 tablespoons fish sauce

2 tablespoons lime juice

3 small fresh red or green chillies, roughly chopped

1 tablespoon finely chopped mint leaves

2 tablespoons ground roasted peanuts

2 tablespoons dry-fried sesame seeds

Bring a pan of water to the boil, add the chicken breast and simmer until cooked through. Drain and leave to cool.

Shred the meat into small pieces into a bowl, allowing any liquid it may retain to fall into the bowl. Add all the remaining ingredients to the chicken and stir well. Turn on to a plate and serve.

Preparation time: 5 minutes   Cooking time: 15 minutes

chilli salmon salad
laab pla

225g (8oz) salmon fillet, broken up with the fingers

2 tablespoons fish sauce

2 tablespoons lemon juice

1 teaspoon sugar

1 teaspoon chilli powder

1 teaspoon finely chopped lemon grass

1 teaspoon finely chopped Kaffir lime leaf

1 spring onion, finely chopped into rings

10 mint leaves

1 head of witloof chicory

Dip the salmon in boiling water to blanch. Remove and drain. Place in a large mixing bowl and add all the remaining ingredients except for the chicory, stirring well.

Arrange the chicory leaves on a serving dish and spoon the chilli salmon mixture on to the leaves just before serving.

Preparation time: 5 minutes   Cooking time: 2 minutes

cucumber and prawn salad
yam taeng gwa

8 raw king prawns, peeled, de-veined and cut in half lengthways

175g (6oz) cucumber, peeled and finely sliced

4 shallots, finely chopped

2 small fresh red chillies, finely chopped

1 medium tomato, cut into segments

2 tablespoons fish sauce

2 tablespoons lemon juice

1 teaspoon sugar

1 tablespoon roast ed sesame seeds

Cook the prawns in boiling water for 3 minutes, then remove and leave to cool.

In a large salad bowl, mix all the remaining ingredients with the cooked prawns. Stir well, turn on to a serving plate and serve.

Preparation time: 3 minutes   Cooking time: 3 minutes

tuna salad
yam platuna

6 large lettuce leaves

115g (4oz) tinned tuna in oil

1 tablespoon finely chopped fresh ginger

1 young lemon grass stalk, thinly sliced

6 small red shallots, thinly sliced

2 small fresh red chillies, finely chopped

1 tablespoon fish sauce

1 tablespoon lime juice

1 teaspoon sugar

2 spring onions, roughly chopped

Arrange the lettuce leaves on a serving platter and set aside. Flake the tuna into a bowl, add all the remaining ingredients and mix well. Turn on to the lettuce-lined platter and serve.

Preparation time: 3 minutes   Cooking time: 0 minutes

beef and aubergine salad
yam nua makua

I first had the idea for this recipe while I was watching a cookery programme on Thai television.

7 round green Thai aubergines, cut in half, then finely sliced

1 teaspoon salt, dissolved in a bowl of water

225g (8oz) tender boneless beef, finely sliced

4 shallots, finely sliced

2 small fresh red chillies, roughly chopped

2 tablespoons fish sauce

1 teaspoon sugar

2 tablespoons lemon juice

20 mint leaves

As you slice the aubergines, place them in the bowl of salted water bowl. This stops the aubergines turning brown. Drain the slices when you are ready to use them.

In a saucepan, heat 4 tablespoons water, then add the beef and cook quickly until the meat is opaque and cooked through. Add the aubergines, shallots, chillies, fish sauce and sugar, stirring briskly. Remove from the heat and add the lemon juice and mint leaves, continuing to stir quickly. Turn the mixture on to a dish and serve.

Preparation time: 5 minutes   Cooking time: 10 minutes

seafood salad
yam talay

2 garlic cloves, very finely chopped

4 small fresh red or green chillies, very finely chopped

2 tablespoons crushed roasted peanuts

1 tablespoon sugar

3 tablespoons fish sauce

3 tablespoons lime juice

Lettuce leaves

1 small onion, thinly sliced and separated into rings

50g (2oz) pineapple segments

50g (2oz) baby squid, chopped into small rings

50g (2oz) raw prawns, peeled, de-veined and halved lengthways

50g (2oz) shelled mussels

50g (2oz) shelled baby clams

50g (2oz) fish balls, halved

Coriander leaves, to garnish

In a bowl, mix the garlic, chillies, peanuts, sugar, fish sauce and lime juice to make a dressing. Set aside. Place the lettuce leaves, onion rings and pineapple segments in a large bowl and set aside.

In a saucepan, heat a cupful of water, add the squid, prawns, mussels and baby clams and cook quickly. Drain, then place all the seafood, including the fish ball halves, into a pan, add the prepared dressing and heat, stirring rapidly for the brief time it takes to cook the ingredients, probably no more than a minute. Turn the mixture into the salad in the large bowl, toss well, garnish with coriander and serve.

Preparation time: 10 minutes   Cooking time: 5 minutes

hot-and-sour pickled cabbage salad
yam pak dong

This can served with rice soup or as a side dish with curries.

175g (6oz) pickled cabbage, finely chopped

2 garlic cloves, finely chopped

4 shallots, finely chopped

4 small fresh hot red or green chillies, finely chopped

1 teaspoon sugar

2 tablespoons roasted peanuts, crushed

In a bowl, mix all the ingredients together. Turn into a serving dish.

Preparation time: 3 minutes   Cooking time: 0 minutes

crispy fish with mango
yam pla krop

In Thailand we use river catfish, which is thin and very easy to crisp.

6 large lettuce leaves
Oil, for deep-frying
3 small red shallots, finely sliced
1 medium trout or similar firm fish, cleaned and filleted

For the dressing
1 green mango, finely sliced into small wedges
1 carrot, cut into 2.5cm (1in) matchsticks
1 celery stalk, cut into 2.5cm (1in) matchsticks
1 tablespoon fish sauce
1 tablespoon lime juice
1 teaspoon sugar
3 small fresh red chillies, finely chopped

Arrange the lettuce leaves on a serving platter and set aside.

Heat the oil and fry the shallots until crispy. Set aside.

Heat 1 tablespoon oil and fry the whole trout fillets until crispy. Drain on kitchen paper, then flake the fish into bite-sized pieces. Place on the lettuce and set aside.

Mix all the dressing ingredients in a bowl, pour over the fish and garnish with the crispy shallots.

Preparation time: 5 minutes   Cooking time: 15 minutes

sweet-and-sour beancurd soup
gaeng preowan tao hou

450ml (16fl oz) vegetable stock
2 teaspoons plain flour
25g (1oz) pickled cabbage, chopped into 2.5cm (1in) lengths
25g (1oz) bamboo shoots, cut into matchsticks
110g (4oz) soft white beancurd, cut into 6mm (1/4in) cubes
25g (1oz) sweet red peppers, deseeded and finely chopped
2 spring onions, finely chopped
2 tablespoons light soy sauce
1 tablespoon vinegar
1 teaspoon sugar
1/2 teaspoon ground white pepper

In a large pan, bring the stock to the boil and stir in the flour to thicken slightly. Add the rest of the ingredients in succession, stirring constantly. Transfer to a serving bowl and serve.

Preparation time: 5 minutes   Cooking time: 5 minutes

cauliflower, coconut and galangal soup
tom ka

125ml (4fl oz) coconut milk
2.5cm (1in) piece of lemon grass, finely chopped into rings
2.5cm (1in) piece of galangal, finely chopped into rings
3 Kaffir lime leaves, roughly torn into quarters
1 small cauliflower, cut into florets
2 tablespoons light soy sauce
1 teaspoon sugar
700ml (1 1/4 pints) vegetable stock
4 small fresh red or green chillies, slightly crushed
2 tablespoons lemon juice
Coriander leaves, to garnish

In a large pan, heat the coconut milk with the lemon grass, galangal, Kaffir lime leaves, cauliflower, soy sauce, sugar and stock and simmer until the cauliflower florets are *al dente*.

Remove from the heat and add the chillies and lemon juice. Stir once, pour into a serving bowl and garnish with coriander leaves.

Preparation time: 5 minutes   Cooking time: 8 minutes

mixed vegetable soup
jap chai

1 garlic clove, roughly chopped
2 coriander roots, roughly chopped
1/2 teaspoon whole black peppercorns
2 tablespoons oil
50g (2oz) white cabbage, finely shredded
50g (2oz) mooli (white radish), cut into 2.5cm (1in) cubes
2 broccoli florets with stems, coarsely chopped
1 celery stalk, coarsely chopped
1.2 litres (2 pints) vegetable stock
110g (4oz) ready-fried beancurd, cut into 2.5cm (1in) cubes
2 tablespoons light soy sauce
1 tablespoon dark soy sauce
1 teaspoon sugar

In a mortar, pound the garlic, coriander roots and peppercorns to form a paste.

In a pan, heat the oil and briefly fry the paste. Add the vegetables and briefly stir-fry. Pour the stock over the vegetables and bring to the boil.

Add all the remaining ingredients and simmer gently until the vegetables are well cooked.

Preparation time: 5 minutes   Cooking time: 10 minutes

vermicelli soup
gaeng wun sen

Beancurd sheets look like wrinkled brown paper and can be bought in packets from Chinese or Thai shops. They are very fragile and should be soaked for 5 minutes before you shred them.

1 garlic clove, finely chopped
1 tablespoon oil
700ml (1 1/4 pints) vegetable stock
50g (2oz) minced pork, roughly shaped into small balls
50g (2oz) pre-soaked dried black fungus mushrooms, coarsely chopped
50g (2oz) beancurd sheet fragments, soaked, then drained
110g (4oz) vermicelli noodles, coarsely chopped
2 spring onions, chopped into 2.5cm (1in) lengths
1 teaspoon tang chi (preserved radish)
1 tablespoon fish sauce
1 tablespoon light soy sauce
1/2 teaspoon sugar
1/2 teaspoon ground white pepper
Coriander leaves, to garnish

Make garlic oil by frying the garlic in the oil until golden brown, then set aside. Bring the stock to the boil, add all the remaining ingredients except the coriander leaves and simmer briefly.

Turn into serving bowls and pour a little garlic oil on to each. Garnish with the coriander leaves.

Preparation time: 5 minutes   Cooking time: 5 minutes

omelette soup
gaeng kaijeow

2 tablespoons oil

1 egg, beaten

700ml (1¼ pints) vegetable stock

1 carrot, chopped into small cubes

1 teaspoon tang chi (preserved radish)

2 spring onions, chopped into 2.5cm (1in) lengths

2 tablespoons light soy sauce

½ teaspoon sugar

½ teaspoon ground white pepper

Coriander leaves, to garnish

Heat the oil in a small omelette pan, add the egg and cook to make a firm omelette. Remove the omelette from the pan, roll into a cylinder and cut into rounds 6mm (¼in) thick. Secure the rounds with a tiny skewer or toothpick and set aside.

Put the stock and carrot into a large pan and bring to the boil. Simmer for 5 minutes, then add all the remaining ingredients except the coriander leaves, ending with the omelette rounds. Stir, then pour into serving bowls and garnish with the coriander leaves.

Preparation time: 10 minutes   Cooking time: 15 minutes

fish ball soup with basil leaves
gaeng krapow

700ml (1¼ pints) chicken stock

1 tablespoon light soy sauce

1 tablespoon fish sauce

1 medium onion, cut in half, then finely sliced

175g (6oz) fish balls

1 small fresh red chilli, finely chopped

15 holy basil leaves

In a saucepan, bring the stock gently to the boil. Add the soy sauce, fish sauce, onion, fish balls and chilli. Cook for 5 minutes, remove from the heat and add the basil leaves.

Ladle the soup into bowls and serve.

Preparation time: 3 minutes   Cooking time: 5 minutes

won ton soup

geo nam

3 garlic cloves, finely chopped

50g (2oz) minced pork

Salt and ground black pepper

6 sheets won ton pastry

450ml (16fl oz) chicken stock

1 teaspoon tang chi (preserved radish)

1 tablespoon fish sauce

1 tablespoon light soy sauce

1/2 teaspoon sugar

1 spring onion, sliced into fine rings

Mix together the garlic, pork and a sprinkling of salt and pepper. Put an equal portion of this mixture in the centre of each won ton sheet. Gather up the corners and squeeze together to make a little purse. Set aside.

In a saucepan, heat the chicken stock and add the preserved radish. Bring to the boil. Add the won ton purses, together with all the remaining ingredients except for the spring onion. Return to the boil, stirring gently.

Remove from the heat and turn into a tureen. Scatter the spring onion rings and a shaking of salt and pepper on top, then serve.

Preparation time: 5 minutes   Cooking time: 5 minutes

prawn soup with sago
gaeng jud sa ku gung

Sago is a starch made from the pith of the sago palm. When boiled the hard, semi-transparent, whitish grains expand into little balls of sweet, transparent jelly.

600ml (1 pint) vegetable stock
2 tablespoons sago
50g (2oz) pre-soaked dried black fungus mushrooms, roughly sliced
1 small onion, sliced into thin strips
1 small carrot, cut into matchsticks
1 teaspoon tang chi (preserved radish)
175g (6oz) raw prawns, peeled and de-veined
2 tablespoons fish sauce
1 teaspoon sugar
$^{1}/_{2}$ teaspoon ground white pepper

For the garnish
1 spring onion, finely chopped into rings
Coriander leaves

In a large pan, bring the stock to the boil, add the sago and simmer until the hard sago 'nuts' have become soft and clear. Add all the remaining ingredients, stirring briefly.

Pour into serving bowls and garnish with the spring onion and coriander leaves.

Preparation time: 5 minutes   Cooking time: 8 minutes

spicy soup with prawns and lemon grass
tom yam kung

This is probably the best-known dish in Thai cooking. *Tom Yam* is a basic method of making soup and you can use it with other ingredients besides prawns: mussels, scallops, crab claws, chicken pieces or thinly sliced beef. The aroma of the soup is created by the main ingredients, a mixture of lemon grass, lime leaves and fresh chilli.

600ml (1 pint) chicken stock
1 lemon grass stalk, chopped into 4 pieces and slightly crushed
4 Kaffir lime leaves, roughly chopped
2 small fresh red chillies, finely sliced
8 small button mushrooms, quartered
8 raw king prawns, peeled and de-veined
2 tablespoons fish sauce
2 tablespoons lime juice
1 teaspoon sugar
Coriander leaves, to garnish

In a saucepan, heat the stock to boiling point. Add the lemon grass, Kaffir lime leaves, chillies and mushrooms and bring back to the boil. Add the prawns, fish sauce, lime juice and sugar and simmer for about a minute or so, until the prawns are cooked.

Turn into soup bowls and garnish with coriander leaves.

Preparation time: 5 minutes   Cooking time: 5 minutes

sweetcorn and shrimp soup
gaeng chud kaopot

500ml (18fl oz) chicken stock
250g (9oz) tinned creamed sweetcorn
175g (6oz) small shrimps
1 egg, beaten
1 tablespoon fish sauce
1 tablespoon soy sauce
1/2 teaspoon black pepper
1 tablespoon chopped coriander leaves

In a large saucepan, bring the chicken stock and corn to the boil. Add the shrimps, pour in the beaten egg and stir to break up the egg in the soup. Add the fish sauce, soy sauce and black pepper. Bring back to the boil and cook for 1 minute.

Pour into a soup tureen, sprinkle with the chopped coriander leaves and serve.

Preparation time: 3 minutes   Cooking time: 5 minutes

hot-and-sour chicken and shallot soup
tom kong

500ml (18fl oz) chicken stock
4 whole chicken wings on the bone, roughly chopped into
  2.5cm (1in) pieces
5 shallots, peeled
2 large dried red chillies
2 tablespoons fish sauce
1 tablespoon lemon juice
1 teaspoon sugar
20 sweet basil leaves

Preheat the grill.

In a saucepan, heat the stock to boiling point. Add the chicken pieces and bring back to the boil, then leave to simmer.

Meanwhile, place the shallots and the chillies under the grill until the chillies start to blacken, turning once. Transfer the grilled shallots and chillies to a board. With the handle or side of a large kitchen knife, crush them until they split open. Add the crushed shallots and chillies to the pan of stock and continue to simmer until the chicken pieces are cooked through.

Add the fish sauce, lemon juice, sugar and basil leaves. Stir quickly and serve at once.

Preparation time: 3 minutes   Cooking time: 15 minutes

soup of minced pork and mushrooms
gaeng chud moo sap

8 whole black peppercorns
2 garlic cloves
3 coriander roots
110g (4oz) minced pork
1.2 litres (2 pints) chicken stock
4 dried Chinese mushrooms, soaked in hot water, de-stemmed and
  finely sliced
1 tablespoon fish sauce
1 tablespoon light soy sauce
2 spring onions, finely chopped

In a mortar, pound the peppercorns, garlic and coriander roots until they form a paste.

In a bowl, mix together the minced pork and the paste until well blended, then form into small balls.

In a saucepan, heat the chicken stock. Add the meatballs, mushrooms, fish sauce and light soy sauce. Bring to the boil, then remove from the heat and add the spring onions just before serving.

Preparation time: 3 minutes   Cooking time: 5 minutes

pork, potato and shallot soup
tom jiew

500ml (18fl oz) chicken stock

175g (6oz) tender boneless pork, cut into 2.5cm (1in) cubes

110g (4oz) potato, cut into 2.5cm (1in) cubes

2 shallots, finely sliced lengthways

1 tablespoon tamarind water

2 tablespoons fish sauce

1 teaspoon sugar

2 small fresh red or green chillies, slightly crushed with the side of a
   kitchen knife

20 sweet basil leaves

In a large pan, heat the chicken stock to boiling point. Add all the
remaining ingredients and simmer until the potato is cooked
al dente. Pour into a tureen and serve.

Preparation time: 8 minutes   Cooking time: 10 minutes

beef with beansprouts
koawleaw nua

1 clove garlic, finely chopped

1 tablespoon oil

850ml (1½ pints) beef stock

2 garlic cloves, roughly crushed

3 coriander roots

1 star anise

225g (8oz) beef fillet, cut into pieces 6mm (¼in) thick

3 tablespoons light soy sauce

2 tablespoons fish sauce

2 teaspoons sugar

½ teaspoon ground white pepper

75g (3oz) beansprouts

1 spring onion, finely chopped, to garnish

First make some garlic oil: fry the garlic in the oil until golden brown,
then set aside.

In a saucepan, heat the stock to boiling point, add the garlic,
coriander roots and star anise and return to the boil. Add the beef,
light soy sauce, fish sauce, sugar and pepper and bring back to the
boil. Then place the beansprouts in the boiling stock for 5 seconds,
stirring well.

Pour the hot soup into serving bowls. Sprinkle with chopped spring
onion and 1 teaspoon of garlic oil.

Preparation time: 5 minutes   Cooking time: 10 minutes

spare rib and tamarind soup
tom som

1 teaspoon whole black peppercorns

1 teaspoon finely chopped coriander root

1 garlic clove, peeled

2 small shallots, peeled

1 tablespoon oil

500ml (18fl oz) chicken stock

450g (1lb) small pork spare ribs, chopped into 2.5cm (1in) pieces

2.5cm (1in) piece of fresh ginger, finely sliced into matchsticks

2 tablespoons tamarind water

1 tablespoon sugar

2 tablespoons fish sauce

2 spring onions, chopped into 2.5cm (1in) lengths

In a mortar, pound together the peppercorns, coriander root, garlic and shallots, until they form a paste.

In a large saucepan, heat the oil and fry the paste for 5 seconds, stirring constantly. Add the stock and bring to the boil, stirring well. Add the spare ribs and bring back to the boil. Add all the remaining ingredients. Return to the boil and simmer for 1 minute. Ladle into bowls and serve.

Preparation time: 5 minutes   Cooking time: 8 minutes

curries &
main dishes

music

Traditional Thai music has unique qualities that cannot be found in any other kind. Its exotic and wondrous sounds are very appealing to foreign visitors. Among the many styles of Thai music that still manage to maintain a traditional air about them are *Luk Thung* and *Mor Lum*. These are the Thai equivalent of 'Country and Western' and, with their distinctive Thai flavour, are hugely popular in rural areas – the photographs opposite and on previous pages show performances of folk music.

Luk Krung is the musical style of the city, and the many new young groups and bands have made this a rapidly growing industry. In fact we have all styles of popular music – jazz, rock, rap, and hip hop.

When I was young I always wanted to be on the stage but my mother wouldn't allow it, telling me that it had no future and no prospects. Nowadays in Thailand parents encourage their children to be entertainers from as young as possible. Teenage boys in country villages dream about becoming either pop singers or Thai boxers (*Muay Thai*), in much the same way as boys in the West want to be pop stars or footballers.

In this chapter, I want to demonstrate the inventiveness of Thai cuisine, and how we have kept the traditions of Thai food alive with modern adaptations. Much as with music, you will find that our food encompasses a wide range of flavours and styles, and is constantly updated and diversified.

Curry pastes

These are the recipes for the curry pastes most commonly used in Thai cooking. You can, of course, buy these pastes ready-made in any Oriental supermarket.

red curry paste
gaeng pet

8 long dried red chillies, deseeded and chopped

1 teaspoon ground coriander seeds

1/2 teaspoon ground cumin seeds

1 teaspoon ground white pepper

2 tablespoons chopped garlic

2 lemon grass stalks

3 coriander roots, chopped

1 teaspoon chopped Kaffir lime zest or finely chopped lime leaves

2.5cm (1in) piece of galangal, chopped

2 teaspoons shrimp paste

1 teaspoon salt

Using a pestle and mortar, or a grinder, blend all the ingredients into a paste. There should be about 4 tablespoons.

Preparation time: 8 minutes   Cooking time: 0 minutes

dry curry paste
gaeng panaeng

10 long dried red chillies, deseeded and chopped

5 shallots, chopped

2 tablespoons chopped garlic

2 lemon grass stalks, chopped

2.5cm (1in) piece of galangal, chopped

1 teaspoon ground coriander seeds

1 teaspoon ground cumin seeds

3 coriander roots, chopped

1 teaspoon shrimp paste

2 tablespoons roasted peanuts

Using a pestle and mortar, or a grinder, blend all the ingredients into a paste. There should be about 6 tablespoons.

Preparation time: 8 minutes   Cooking time: 0 minutes

green curry paste
gaeng keow wan

2 long fresh green chillies, chopped

10 small fresh green chillies, chopped

1 tablespoon chopped lemon grass

3 shallots, chopped

2 tablespoons chopped garlic

2.5cm (1in) piece of galangal, chopped

3 coriander roots, chopped

1 teaspoon ground coriander seeds

$^1/_2$ teaspoon ground cumin seeds

$^1/_2$ teaspoon ground white pepper

1 teaspoon chopped Kaffir lime zest or finely chopped lime leaves

2 teaspoons shrimp paste

1 teaspoon salt

Using a pestle and mortar, or a grinder, blend all the ingredients into a paste. There should be about 3 tablespoons.

Preparation time: 8 minutes   Cooking time: 0 minutes

vegetable curry
gaeng pa

2 tablespoons oil

1 tablespoon red curry paste (see page 72)

25g (1oz) krachai, peeled and cut into matchsticks

500ml (18fl oz) vegetable stock

50g (2oz) long beans, cut into 2.5cm (1in) pieces

50g (2oz) carrots, cut into matchsticks

50g (2oz) baby sweetcorn, cut into 2.5cm (1in) pieces

3 Kaffir lime leaves, roughly chopped

2 large fresh red or green chillies, roughly chopped

2 tablespoons light soy sauce

1 teaspoon sugar

1/2 teaspoon salt

4 round green Thai aubergines, quartered

20 basil leaves

In a saucepan, heat the oil and quickly stir in the curry paste. Add the krachai and the vegetable stock and stir briefly, then add all the remaining ingredients except the basil. Stir well. Add the basil leaves, stir once, then turn into a bowl and serve.

Preparation time: 5 minutes   Cooking time: 5 minutes

potato curry
gaeng kari

1 teaspoon coriander seeds

2 teaspoons finely chopped galangal

2 teaspoons finely chopped lemon grass

2 teaspoons finely chopped garlic

2 tablespoons oil

225ml (8fl oz) coconut milk

225g (8oz) potatoes, cut into 2.5cm (1in) cubes

2 tablespoons light soy sauce

1 teaspoon sugar

1/2 teaspoon salt

1 tablespoon curry powder

125ml (4fl oz) vegetable stock

225g (8oz) small onions, halved

In a mortar, pound the coriander seeds, galangal, lemon grass and garlic together to form a paste.

In a saucepan, heat the oil, stir in the paste and immediately add the coconut milk. Stir briefly, then add the potatoes, soy sauce, sugar, salt and curry powder; stir well. Bring to the boil and add the vegetable stock. Return to the boil, add the onion halves and simmer until the potatoes are cooked *al dente*.

Preparation time: 5 minutes   Cooking time: 10 minutes

spicy quick-fried long beans
pat prik king

Oil, for deep-frying, plus 2 tablespoons
90g (3oz) beancurd, finely sliced
1 teaspoon finely chopped garlic
1 tablespoon red curry paste (see page 72)
225g (8oz) long beans, cut into 2.5cm (1in) pieces
2 tablespoons light soy sauce
4 tablespoons vegetable stock
1 teaspoon sugar
1 tablespoon ground roasted peanuts
2 Kaffir lime leaves, finely chopped

Deep-fry the beancurd in hot oil until the white sides are golden brown, drain and set aside.

In a wok or frying pan, heat 2 tablespoons oil, fry the garlic until golden brown, then stir in the red curry paste. Add all the remaining ingredients, finishing with the beancurd. Stir briefly and serve.

Preparation time: 5 minutes   **Cooking time: 15 minutes**

sweet-and-sour vegetables
pat preow wan

1 teaspoon cornflour
2 tablespoons oil
1 teaspoon finely chopped garlic
2 baby sweetcorn
8–10 pineapple chunks
1 small chunk cucumber, quartered, then cut into thick slices
1 onion, halved, then sliced into thin segments
1 tomato, quartered
2 medium spring onions, cut into 2.5cm (1in) lengths
2 large fresh red chillies, sliced on the diagonal
2 tablespoons light soy sauce
1 teaspoon sugar
1/2 teaspoon ground white pepper

Mix the cornflour with 4 tablespoons water and set aside.

In a wok or frying pan, heat the oil and fry the garlic until golden brown. Add each of the remaining ingredients in succession, stirring constantly. Add the cornflour and water mix, stirring briefly to thicken, and turn on to a serving dish.

Preparation time: 5 minutes   **Cooking time: 5 minutes**

fried bamboo shoots with egg
pat normai

2 tablespoons oil

1 teaspoon finely chopped garlic

110g (4oz) skinless chicken breast, finely sliced

1 egg

225g (8oz) bamboo shoots, diagonally sliced 6mm (¼in) thick

1 onion, halved, then chopped into thin slices

2 medium spring onions, finely chopped into rings

60g (2oz) oyster mushrooms, thinly sliced

1 tablespoon light soy sauce

1 tablespoon fish sauce

½ teaspoon sugar

½ teaspoon ground white pepper

Coriander leaves, to garnish

In a wok or frying pan, heat the oil and fry the garlic until golden brown. Add the chicken stir and cook until the meat is slightly opaque. Break the egg into the pan, spreading the broken yolk a little. Before the egg sets, throw in the bamboo shoots, onion, spring onions and mushrooms and stir rapidly. Add the remaining ingredients (except the coriander leaves), continuing to stir rapidly, and turn on to a serving dish. Garnish with the coriander leaves.

Preparation time: 3 minutes   Cooking time: 15 minutes

mushrooms with ginger
pat king

2 tablespoons oil

1 teaspoon finely chopped garlic

50g (2oz) pre-soaked dried black fungus mushrooms, coarsely chopped if large

1 onion, halved, then chopped into thin slices

1 carrot, cut lengthways into thin strips

½ sweet red pepper, cut lengthways into thin strips

5cm (2in) piece of fresh ginger, cut into fine matchsticks

2 medium spring onions, finely chopped

1 tablespoon light soy sauce

1 teaspoon yellow bean sauce

½ teaspoon sugar

4 tablespoons vegetable stock

Coriander leaves, to garnish

In a wok or frying pan, heat the oil and fry the garlic until golden brown. Add all the remaining ingredients (except the coriander leaves) in succession, stirring constantly. Turn on to a serving dish and garnish with the coriander.

Preparation time: 5 minutes   Cooking time: 3 minutes

morning glory curry
gaeng te po

Morning glory (water spinach) has a taste that is similar to spinach and is a common ingredient in Thai cooking. It is easily recognisable by its arrow-shaped leaves.

2 tablespoons oil
1 garlic clove, finely chopped
1 tablespoon red curry paste (see page 72)
225ml (8fl oz) coconut milk
110g (4oz) oyster mushrooms, chopped
110g (4oz) ready-fried beancurd, sliced into 5 x 1.25cm
  (2 x 1/2in) strips
3 Kaffir lime leaves, coarsely chopped
1 small Kaffir lime, halved
1/2 teaspoon salt
1 tablespoon tamarind water (or 2 tablespoons lemon juice)
1 tablespoon light soy sauce
1 teaspoon sugar
125ml (4fl oz) vegetable stock
1 bunch of morning glory (water spinach), chopped into 2.5cm
  (1in) lengths

In a frying pan or wok, heat the oil and fry the garlic until golden brown. Stir in the curry paste and immediately add the coconut milk, stirring well. Add the remaining ingredients in succession, except the stock and morning glory, stirring constantly. Bring to the boil, add the vegetable stock and return to the boil. Add the morning glory and simmer until cooked.

Preparation time: 10 minutes   Cooking time: 8 minutes

pork curry with morning glory
pra ram rong song

175g (6oz) morning glory (water spinach), chopped into 5cm
  (2in) lengths
225g (8oz) boneless lean pork, finely slivered
2 tablespoons oil
2 garlic cloves, finely chopped
1 tablespoon dry curry paste (see page 73)
1 tablespoon fish sauce
1 tablespoon light soy sauce
1 teaspoon sugar
5 tablespoons coconut milk
2 tablespoons ground roasted peanuts

Bring a pan of water to the boil, blanch the morning glory for 2 minutes, drain, reserving the cooking water, and arrange on a serving dish. Cook the pork in the reserved water for about 5 minutes, drain and arrange on the morning glory, and set aside.

In a frying pan, heat the oil and fry the garlic until golden brown. Add the curry paste, fish sauce, light soy sauce and sugar and mix thoroughly. Then add the coconut milk and ground roasted peanuts, stirring well. Bring to the boil, pour over the pork and morning glory and serve.

Preparation time: 5 minutes   Cooking time: 15 minutes

fried fish with chillies and tamarind sauce
pla lat prik

2 large garlic cloves, finely chopped
2 large fresh red chillies, finely chopped
1 medium firm-fleshed fish suitable for deep-frying (such as bream or sea bass)
Oil, for deep-frying, plus 2 tablespoons
2 tablespoons palm sugar or white sugar
3 tablespoons fish sauce
2 tablespoons tamarind water (or 4 tablespoons lemon juice)

In a mortar, pound the garlic and chillies together. Set aside.

Rinse the fish and pat dry. Heat a pan of oil for deep-frying, then fry the fish until golden and crispy. Drain and place on a serving dish. Keep hot.

Heat 2 tablespoons oil in a wok or frying pan, then stir in the garlic and chilli mix. Add the palm sugar and stir, then stir in the fish sauce and tamarind water. Pour over the fish and serve.

Preparation time: 5 minutes   Cooking time: 10 minutes

crab with chilli
bu pad prik

4 fresh medium crabs
1 tablespoon finely chopped ginger
3 garlic cloves, finely chopped
4 fresh red or green chillies, finely chopped
4 tablespoons oil
2 tomatoes, sliced
1 tablespoon fish sauce
1 tablespoon light soy sauce
1 teaspoon sugar

First prepare the crabs. Remove the undershell and discard the abdominal sac just behind the mouth. Break off the pincers and crack them open. With a Chinese chopper, quarter each crab. Set aside.

In a mortar, pound together the ginger, garlic and chillies to make a paste. Heat the oil in a wok or deep frying pan and stir in the paste. Stir in the tomatoes and 2 tablespoons water. Add the crab pieces, fish sauce, soy sauce and sugar and stir well, ensuring that the crab is cooked and the pieces are well coated. Turn on to a platter and serve.

Preparation time: 10 minutes   Cooking time: 10 minutes

baby clams with dry curry
hoy pat pet

2 tablespoons oil

2 garlic cloves, finely chopped

2 teaspoons red curry paste (see page 72)

450g (1lb) baby clams in the shell

2 tablespoons fish sauce

1 tablespoon light soy sauce

1 teaspoon sugar

3 round green Thai aubergines, quartered
  (Western aubergine can be used)

2 small Kaffir lime leaves, finely sliced

10 holy basil leaves

In a wok or frying pan, heat the oil, add the garlic and fry until golden brown. Add the curry paste, mix and cook for a few seconds.

Now add the baby clams and cook briefly. Stirring constantly, add the remaining ingredients, pausing after the addition of the aubergines to give them a few seconds to cook.

When the clams are cooked through and opaque, give a final stir, pour the mixture on to a warmed dish, and serve.

Preparation time: 5 minutes   Cooking time: 5 minutes

scallops with vegetables and oyster sauce
hoy pad nam mun hoy

2 tablespoons oil

2 garlic cloves, finely chopped

8 scallops, shelled

50g (2oz) baby sweetcorn, quartered

50g (2oz) broccoli, chopped into small florets

50g (2oz) celery, finely sliced

50g (2oz) carrots, cut into matchsticks

2 tablespoons oyster sauce

1/2 teaspoon sugar

Ground white pepper, to taste

In a frying pan, heat the oil and fry the garlic until golden brown. Add the scallops and briefly stir-fry. Then add all the remaining ingredients in succession, except the pepper, stirring well between each addition. Sprinkle with the pepper and serve.

Preparation time: 5 minutes   Cooking time: 5 minutes

prawns with holy basil
kung pad krapow

This recipe can be adapted by substituting pork or chicken for the prawns, but the meat should be very finely chopped, or even coarsely minced.

2 tablespoons oil
2 garlic cloves, finely chopped
2 small fresh red or green chillies, finely chopped
6–8 raw king prawns, peeled and de-veined
1 medium onion, halved and roughly sliced
2 tablespoons fish sauce
1 tablespoons light soy sauce
1 teaspoon sugar
20 holy basil leaves

In a wok or frying pan, heat the oil and fry the garlic and chillies, stirring well, until the garlic begins to brown. Add the prawns and stir, then add the remaining ingredients, mixing well. Cook until the prawns are opaque and cooked through. Turn on to a dish and serve.

Preparation time: 5 minutes   Cooking time: 10 minutes

fried prawns with red curry paste
chu chee kung

2 large dried red chillies, finely chopped
8 small red shallots, finely chopped
1 tablespoon red curry paste (see page 72)
2 tablespoons oil
2 tablespoons roasted peanuts, crushed
225g (8oz) raw prawns, peeled and de-veined
225g (8oz) long beans, cut into 2.5cm (1in) lengths
125ml (4fl oz) coconut milk
1/2 teaspoon salt
1 teaspoon sugar

In a mortar, pound together the chillies and shallots. Add the curry paste and mix well.

Heat the oil in a wok or frying pan and briefly fry the paste. Add the peanuts and prawns. Stir well, until the prawns are opaque and cooked through, then add the long beans, coconut milk, salt and sugar. Stir well for a few seconds, then turn into a bowl and serve.

Preparation time: 5 minutes   Cooking time: 5 minutes

steamed fish with lemon grass
pla neung ta-krai

1 sea bass (about 450g/1lb), scored with diagonal cuts on both sides
4 lemon grass stalks, roughly crushed
Coriander leaves, to garnish

For the sauce
4 garlic cloves, finely chopped
3 small fresh red or green chillies, finely chopped
3 tablespoons fish sauce
4 tablespoons lime juice
2 teaspoons sugar

Place the fish on a bed of lemon grass on a steaming tray, and steam over boiling water for about 15 minutes until cooked.

To make the sauce, combine the garlic, chillies, fish sauce, lime juice and sugar in a bowl.

To serve, arrange the fish on a serving dish, pour the sauce over and garnish with coriander leaves.

Preparation time: 5 minutes   Cooking time: 15 minutes

fried chilli prawns with tamarind sauce
kung makham

2 tablespoons oil
1 large garlic clove, finely chopped
2 teaspoons grated fresh ginger
1 large fresh red chilli, cut into small strips
2 tablespoons tamarind water (or 4 tablespoons lemon juice)
1 tablespoon sugar
20 raw tiger prawns, peeled and de-veined
2 tablespoons fish sauce
Coriander leaves, to garnish

In a wok or frying pan, heat the oil and fry the garlic until golden. Add the ginger, chilli, tamarind water and sugar, stirring well. Add the prawns and fish sauce, stirring well until the prawns are opaque and cooked through.

Turn on to a serving dish, garnish with the coriander and serve.

Preparation time: 5 minutes   Cooking time: 5 minutes

chicken curry with bamboo shoots
gaeng normai gai

2 tablespoons vegetable oil
1 large garlic clove, finely chopped
1 tablespoon red curry paste (see page 72)
225ml (8fl oz) coconut milk
2 tablespoons fish sauce
1 teaspoon sugar
175g (6oz) boneless chicken, finely sliced
125ml (4fl oz) chicken stock
110g (4oz) bamboo shoots, cut into thin slices
3 Kaffir lime leaves, finely sliced
3 large fresh red chillies, sliced lengthways
20 holy basil leaves

In a wok or frying pan, heat the oil and fry the garlic until golden brown. Add the curry paste and cook briefly, stirring well. Stir in half the coconut milk, the fish sauce and the sugar. Add the chicken and stir well, then add the chicken stock and bamboo shoots. Stir again. Add the remaining coconut milk, the lime leaves and the chillies. Stir and cook until the chicken is cooked through.

Add the basil leaves, stir and cook gently for 1 minute, then turn into a serving dish.

Preparation time: 5 minutes   Cooking time: 5 minutes

chicken fried with cashew nuts and dried chillies
gai pad med mamuang hin ma pan

2 tablespoons oil
2 garlic cloves, finely chopped
225g (8oz) skinless chicken breast, finely sliced
1 tablespoon fish sauce
4 long dried chillies, cut into rounds
2 heaped tablespoons roasted cashews
1 tablespoon oyster sauce
1/2 teaspoon sugar

In a frying pan, heat the oil and fry the garlic until golden brown. Add the chicken, stir and cook until the meat is slightly opaque.

Stirring after each addition, add the remaining ingredients, cook until the chicken is cooked through and serve.

Preparation time: 3 minutes   Cooking time: 6 minutes

southern chicken curry

gaeng kolae

Kolae is the name of the boats used by fishermen in the south of Thailand, which is where this dish originates.

4 tablespoons oil
2 large garlic cloves, finely chopped
1 chicken weighing 1.3–1.8kg (3–4lb), roughly chopped, with skin
  and bones, into 10–12 large pieces
450ml (16fl oz) coconut cream
500ml (18fl oz) chicken stock
4 tablespoons fish sauce
2 tablespoons sugar
4 tablespoons lime juice
10 small fresh red or green chillies, thinly sliced, to garnish

For the curry paste
5 large dried red chillies, deseeded and soaked in water for 5 minutes
^{1}/2 teaspoon salt
1 teaspoon roughly chopped lemon grass
^{1}/2 teaspoon coriander seeds
^{1}/2 teaspoon cumin seeds
1 teaspoon dried shrimp paste

To make the curry paste, place all the ingredients in a mortar and pound together.

In a wok or frying pan, heat the oil and fry the garlic until golden brown. Add the chicken and fry until golden. Remove from the oil and set aside.

Pour the oil from the wok into a large saucepan, heat and add the prepared paste, stirring until it begins to blend. Add half the coconut cream and stir well, then add the browned chicken and mix thoroughly. Add the remaining coconut cream and stir, add the chicken stock and fish sauce and stir, add the sugar and lime juice and stir well, bringing the liquid to the boil. Reduce the heat and simmer for 15 minutes.

Turn into a bowl and serve garnished with the chillies.

Preparation time: 10 minutes   Cooking time: 20 minutes

chicken pineapple curry
gaeng kua sapparot

1 tablespoon oil

2 garlic cloves, finely chopped

1 tablespoon red curry paste (see page 72)

175g (6oz) boneless chicken, finely sliced

300ml (1/2 pint) coconut milk

1 small fresh pineapple, peeled, cored and cut into small segments

3 Kaffir lime leaves, finely chopped

2 tablespoons lemon juice

2 teaspoons sugar

1 teaspoon salt

In a wok or frying pan, heat the oil and fry the garlic until golden brown. Add the curry paste and chicken and fry briefly, stirring, then add the coconut milk, stirring well. Slowly bring to the boil, then add the remaining ingredients, stirring constantly until the chicken is cooked through. Turn into a bowl and serve.

Preparation time: 5 minutes   Cooking time: 10 minutes

chicken curry with pickled garlic
gaeng haeng lay

1 tablespoon oil

1 tablespoon red curry paste (see page 72)

175g (6oz) boneless chicken, roughly sliced

1/2 teaspoon ground turmeric

4 tablespoons coconut cream

2 tablespoons water

75g (3oz) pre-soaked dried Chinese mushrooms, coarsely chopped

1 tablespoon lemon juice

1 tablespoon fish sauce

1 teaspoon sugar

1/2 teaspoon salt

2.5cm (1in) piece of fresh ginger, cut into matchsticks

1 whole head of pickled garlic, finely sliced across the bulb to make flower-shaped sections

In a wok or frying pan, heat the oil and briefly stir in the curry paste. Add all the other ingredients in succession, stirring briefly between each addition. Once the chicken is cooked through, immediately turn into a bowl and serve.

Preparation time: 5 minutes   Cooking time: 10 minutes

beef with asparagus and oyster sauce

nua pad nam man hoy

2 tablespoons oil

2 garlic cloves, finely chopped

175g (6oz) beef, thinly sliced

175g (6oz) young thin asparagus, chopped into 5cm (2in) lengths
 (or any other crunchy vegetable such as broccoli)

2 tablespoons oyster sauce

1 tablespoon fish sauce

1/2 teaspoon sugar

1/2 teaspoon ground white pepper

In a wok or frying pan, heat the oil and fry the garlic until golden brown. Stirring constantly, add each of the remaining ingredients in succession, stirring well between each addition. When the beef is cooked, turn on to a serving dish and serve.

Preparation time: 5 minutes   Cooking time: 5 minutes

green beef curry
gaeng keow wan nua

This is my mother's recipe, and whenever I eat it I think of her.

2 tablespoons oil
2 garlic cloves, finely chopped
1 tablespoon green curry paste (see page 73)
225g (8oz) tender boneless beef steak, finely sliced, retaining the fat
225ml (8fl oz) coconut cream
225ml (8fl oz) beef stock
2 large fresh red chillies, sliced diagonally into thin ovals
2 tablespoons fish sauce
6 round green Thai aubergines, quartered
1 teaspoon sugar
20 sweet basil leaves

In a large saucepan, heat the oil and fry the garlic until golden brown. Stir in the curry paste, mixing well. Add the beef and stir-fry until just cooked through. Add the coconut cream and stir well, bringing to the boil. Add the stock and return to the boil, stirring constantly. Simmer for 5 minutes, stirring in all the remaining ingredients except the basil. Stir in the basil leaves just before pouring the curry into a serving bowl.

Preparation time: 5 minutes   Cooking time: 10 minutes

beef panaeng curry
gaeng panaeng

As the name suggests, this dish is of Malaysian origin, and is drier than most Thai curries.

125ml (4fl oz) coconut cream, plus 1 tablespoon for garnish
2 tablespoons oil
1 garlic clove, finely chopped
1 tablespoon dry curry paste (see page 73)
175g (6oz) lean beef, diced
2 tablespoons fish sauce
1 teaspoon sugar
2 Kaffir lime leaves, very finely chopped
15 holy basil leaves
1 long fresh red chilli, sliced lengthways

In a small pan, gently heat the 125ml (4fl oz) coconut cream, but do not let it boil; set aside.

In a wok or frying pan, heat the oil until a light haze appears, add the garlic and fry until golden brown.

Add the curry paste and stir-fry for a few seconds. Add the beef and stir-fry until it is lightly cooked. Add the hot coconut cream, stir well, then add the fish sauce and sugar, continuing to stir. Just before serving stir in the lime leaves, holy basil and chilli. Turn into a bowl and garnish with 1 tablespoon coconut cream.

Preparation time: 5 minutes   Cooking time: 5 minutes

stuffed omelette
kai yat sai

1 tablespoon oil
2 garlic cloves, finely chopped
110g (4oz) minced pork
50g (2oz) onions, finely chopped
50g (2oz) carrots, finely diced
50g (2oz) green peas
1 tomato, finely diced
2 tablespoons fish sauce
1/2 teaspoon sugar
Pinch of ground black pepper

For the omelette
2 eggs
1 tablespoon oil

Heat the oil and fry the garlic until golden brown. Add the minced pork, stirring well. Add all the remaining ingredients in succession, stirring constantly. Remove from the heat and set aside.

To make the omelette, beat the eggs. In a wok, heat the oil, turning the wok so that the oil coats the entire inner surface. Pour in the eggs and turn to spread evenly. When the egg has cooked, pour the pork filling into the centre. Fold in the sides of the omelette to make a square parcel. Cook for a moment longer, then lift carefully on to a dish to serve.

Preparation time: 10 minutes   Cooking time: 8 minutes

pork with garlic and peppercorns
moo tod kratiam prik thai sod

This dish is somewhat different from the norm in Thai cuisine as it derives its heat from peppercorns rather than from chillies.

2 tablespoons oil
2 large garlic cloves, finely chopped
110g (4oz) lean pork, finely chopped
1 tablespoon fish sauce
1 tablespoon light soy sauce
1 tablespoon dark soy sauce
4 tablespoons meat stock or water
Pinch of ground white pepper
10 fresh peppercorns

In a wok or frying pan, heat the oil until a light haze appears. Add the garlic and fry until golden brown. Add the pork and cook briefly, stirring constantly. Add the remaining ingredients one by one, stirring briefly between each addition. By now the pork should be cooked through. Turn the heat up for a few seconds to reduce the liquid to about 3 tablespoons.

Turn on to a serving dish and serve.

Preparation time: 3 minutes   Cooking time: 5 minutes

spicy beancurd with minced pork
chu chee tao hou

This recipe can be made vegetarian by omitting the meat, substituting light soy sauce for fish sauce, and using vegetable stock instead of chicken stock.

Oil, for deep-frying, plus 2 tablespoons
225g (8oz) beancurd, cut into 1cm (1/2in) cubes
1 tablespoon red curry paste (see page 72)
110g (4oz) minced pork
2 tablespoons fish sauce
1 teaspoon sugar
4 tablespoons chicken stock
2 Kaffir lime leaves, rolled up into a thin cylinder and sliced into fine slivers

Heat a pan of oil for deep-frying. Deep-fry the beancurd cubes until golden brown. Drain on kitchen paper and arrange on a serving dish. Set aside.

Heat 2 tablespoons oil in a wok or frying pan and briefly fry the curry paste, stirring constantly. Add the minced pork and stir-fry until it is no longer pink. Add the fish sauce, sugar and stock, mixing well.

Add the Kaffir lime leaf slivers. Pour the sauce over the deep-fried beancurd and serve.

Preparation time: 3 minutes   Cooking time: 3 minutes

fried pork with aubergine
moo pad makua

This is my favourite dish and I often order it in restaurants. I am generally able to judge the standard of the food there by how they cook this dish.

2 tablespoons oil
2 garlic cloves, finely chopped
4 small fresh red or green chillies, finely chopped
175g (6oz) minced pork
225g (8oz) long Thai aubergines, roughly sliced (or purple aubergines, thinly sliced)
2 tablespoons fish sauce
1 teaspoon sugar
20 sweet basil leaves

Heat the oil in a wok or frying pan and fry the garlic until golden brown. Add the chillies and stir well. Add the pork, stir, then add the aubergines. Stir again, add the fish sauce and sugar, then stir-fry until the aubergine is just cooked through.

Add the basil leaves, stir thoroughly, then turn on to a dish and serve.

Preparation time: 5 minutes   Cooking time: 5 minutes

minced pork with curry paste and bamboo shoots
moo kua kling normai

2 tablespoons oil

2 garlic cloves, finely chopped

1 tablespoon red curry paste (see page 72)

¹/₂ teaspoon ground turmeric

175g (6oz) minced pork

110g (4oz) bamboo shoots, finely sliced

1 tablespoon fish sauce

1 tablespoon light soy sauce

1 teaspoon sugar

5 Kaffir lime leaves, rolled up into a thin cylinder and finely sliced

In a frying pan, heat the oil and fry the garlic until golden brown. Add the curry paste, turmeric and minced pork and stir-fry until the meat is cooked through.

Add the bamboo shoots, fish sauce, light soy sauce and sugar, and mix thoroughly. At the last moment, stir in the Kaffir lime leaves and turn on to a serving dish.

Preparation time: 3 minutes   Cooking time: 3 minutes

noodles & rice

thai films

Thai cinemas now show the best of Thai, Chinese and Western films. This cultural mix reminds me of my close friend, the film producer Tom Waller, who is half Thai and half English.

He recently worked on the production of Oliver Stone's *Alexander*, a multi-million dollar epic movie about Alexander the Great that was partly filmed in Lopburi, Thailand.

With more than 500 local crew and hundreds of Thai soldiers playing Macedonian warriors, blockbuster films like this help to support the Thai film industry. But for about the same cost as *Alexander's* catering budget for the extras alone, Tom Waller produced an independent movie in Thailand called *Butterfly Man*, an adventure about a young Englishman who falls in love with Thai massage, Thai cooking and a beautiful Thai woman, played by newcomer Napakpapha Mamee Nakprasitte, who won a Best Actress award at a US film festival in 2003. Accolades like these have helped to put Thai talent on the movie-making map.

Most indigenous Thai films are rarely successful abroad; however, several new directors are making their mark at film festivals around the world. Influential directors such as Nonzee Nimibutr and Penek Ratanaruang have pioneered a new wave of modern Thai cinema, and are often critically acclaimed overseas before they are at home.

The catering on Thai film sets usually consists of a quick lunch, served in takeaway boxes. They are usually single-dish meals, based on rice and noodles, but I want to show you that there is far more than just pineapple fried rice and pad thai – here are exciting combinations and a wide range of flavours using the many types of noodles, steamed and sticky rice, vegetables, seafood and meat.

rice
khao

Rice is the all-important food in Thailand. In the Thai language the verb 'to eat' is *Kin khao*, which actually means 'eat rice'. Rice is completely central to Thai food. A Thai will always start by having a plate of rice; the other dishes are to accompany the rice, not vice versa as in the West. Thais will also feel uncomfortable if they don't eat rice once a day, no matter what else they may have eaten.

Traditionally we Thais finish all the rice on our plate out of respect for the Mother Goddess of Rice and to acknowledge the hardship that farmers endure in cultivating their crop. After finishing the meal, appreciative diners will put their hands together to thank the rice for filling their stomachs.

The recipes in this chapter deal with variations on the fried-rice dishes that are popular throughout Thailand. Fried rice serves as a gentle introduction to Thai cuisine for the gastronomically timid and those unused to highly spiced foods. *Kao Pad* (fried rice) is eaten for a quick meal at any time of the day.

boiled rice
khao suay

An experienced Thai cook varies the water quantity according to the age, and thus the dryness, of the rice; the amount below is a reasonable average.

450g (1lb) Thai fragrant rice
600ml (1 pint) water

Rinse the rice thoroughly in at least three changes of cold water, until the water runs clear. Drain the rice and put it in a heavy saucepan with the measured water. Cover and quickly bring to the boil. Uncover and cook, stirring vigorously, until the water level is below that of the rice, whose surface will begin to look dry. Reduce the heat to as low as possible, cover the pan again and steam for 20 minutes.

Alternatively, buy a rice cooker – they are cheap, efficient, and make and keep perfect rice with absolutely no fuss or bother.

crispy rice
khao tang

If, when you are cooking the rice, a mishap occurs and you are left with rice sticking to the bottom of the pan, don't worry: nothing is wasted in Thai cooking. Let the pan cool down then lift out the sheet of rice and dry it. Break it into three or four pieces. Heat a pan of oil for deep-frying and fry the rice pieces until they are golden brown and crisp. Drain on kitchen paper.

sticky or glutinous rice
khao niew

This is a broad short-grain rice, mostly white, although it can be brown, or even black. It is the staple of northern Thailand, where during the meal it is plucked with the fingers, rolled into a ball and used to scoop up the other food. It is also used throughout Thailand to make sweets. Sticky rice cannot be cooked in a rice cooker, and needs to be soaked before cooking.

steamed sticky rice
khao niew neung

450g (1lb) sticky rice

Put the rice in a pan, cover with water and soak for at least 3 hours, or overnight if possible. Drain and rinse thoroughly. Line the perforated part of a steamer with a double thickness of muslin or cheesecloth and turn the rice into it. Heat the water in the bottom of the steamer to boiling and steam the rice over a moderate heat for 30 minutes.

vegetarian fried rice
khao pad mang sa virad

2 tablespoons oil

2 garlic cloves, finely chopped

6 tablespoons mixed cooked beans, e.g. mangetout and runner beans

2 tablespoons diced carrots

2 tablespoons diced tomato

2 tablespoons diced pineapple

2 tablespoons light soy sauce

1 teaspoon sugar

1/2 teaspoon ground white pepper

225g (8oz) boiled fragrant rice (see page 106)

Coriander leaves, to garnish

In a wok or frying pan, heat the oil and fry the garlic until golden brown. Stirring constantly, add each of the remaining ingredients in succession, (except for the coriander). Stir thoroughly, until the rice is heated through, then turn on to a serving dish and garnish with the coriander leaves.

Preparation time: 3 minutes   Cooking time: 5 minutes

pineapple fried rice
khao pad supparot

2 tablespoons oil

2 tablespoons dried shrimp

2 garlic cloves, finely chopped

450g (1lb) boiled fragrant rice (see page 106)

1 tablespoon fish sauce

1 tablespoon light soy sauce

1 teaspoon sugar

1 small pineapple, chopped into 1cm (1/2in) cubes (reserve the shell)

3 shallots, coarsely chopped

1 large fresh red chilli, finely sliced

1 spring onion, coarsely chopped

1 sprig of coriander, coarsely chopped, plus leaves, to garnish

In a wok or frying pan, heat 1 tablespoon of the oil, add the dried shrimp and fry until crispy. With a slotted spoon, remove the shrimp, drain and set aside.

Add the remaining oil to the wok, heat, add the garlic and fry until golden brown. Add the cooked rice and stir thoroughly.

Add the fish sauce, soy sauce and sugar. Stir and mix thoroughly. Make sure the rice is heated through, then add the pineapple, shallots, chilli, spring onion, coriander and the crispy shrimp. Mix thoroughly and heat through.

Fill the pineapple shell with the mixture, garnish with the coriander leaves and serve.

Preparation time: 5 minutes   Cooking time: 5 minutes

fried rice with mushrooms and pickled cabbage
khao pad pak gat dong

2 tablespoons oil

2 garlic cloves, finely chopped

450g (1lb) boiled fragrant rice (see page 106)

110g (4oz) firm mushrooms (such as oyster mushrooms),
 coarsely chopped

175g (6oz) pickled cabbage

1 tablespoon light soy sauce

1 teaspoon sugar

Black pepper, to taste

Heat the oil in a wok or large frying pan and fry the garlic until golden brown. Then add all the remaining ingredients and stir-fry for about 30 seconds, before turning out on to a serving dish.

Preparation time: 3 minutes   Cooking time: 3 minutes

fried rice with turmeric
khao pad kamin

2 tablespoons oil

1 garlic clove, finely chopped

1 small onion, diced

1 carrot, diced

1 teaspoon ground turmeric

225g (8oz) boiled fragrant rice (see page 106)

1/2 teaspoon sugar

3 teaspoons light soy sauce

1/2 teaspoon chilli powder

50g (2oz) ready-fried beancurd, quartered

For the garnish

1 spring onion, finely chopped

1 medium tomato, cut into wedges

7.5cm (3in) piece of cucumber, cut into 2.5cm (1/2in) slices

In a wok or frying pan, heat the oil until a light haze appears. Add the garlic and fry until golden brown. Stirring constantly, add the onion, carrot, turmeric and rice. Stir thoroughly. Add the sugar, light soy sauce and chilli powder. Stir thoroughly.

Add the beancurd, stir and turn on to a serving dish. Sprinkle with the spring onion rings and arrange the tomato and cucumber at the side of the dish.

Preparation time: 3 minutes   Cooking time: 5 minutes

chicken with mushrooms and bamboo shoots on rice

khao na gai

450g (1lb) boiled fragrant rice (see page 106)

2 tablespoons oil

2 garlic cloves, finely chopped

110g (4oz) boneless chicken, finely sliced

50g (2oz) bamboo shoots, sliced

50g (2oz) straw mushrooms, halved

1 tablespoon light soy sauce

2 tablespoons fish sauce

1 teaspoon sugar

1 tablespoon dark soy sauce

4 tablespoons chicken stock or water

1 tablespoon plain flour, mixed with 2 tablespoons water

2 spring onions, roughly chopped

Pinch of ground white pepper

Put the cooked rice on a serving dish and keep warm. Heat the oil in a wok or frying pan and fry the garlic until golden brown. Add the chicken and stir-fry for a few seconds. Add the bamboo shoots and straw mushrooms and stir. Stirring quickly after each addition, add the light soy sauce, fish sauce, sugar, dark soy sauce and stock. Add more stock if the mixture becomes dry.

Add 1 tablespoon of the flour and water mixture to the wok and stir until thoroughly blended to make a slightly thickened sauce, adding a little more stock or flour/water mixture if necessary.

Add the chopped spring onions and pepper, stir quickly and serve immediately over the cooked rice.

Preparation time: 5 minutes   **Cooking time: 5 minutes**

spicy fried rice with chicken
khao pad prik gai

2 tablespoons oil

2 garlic cloves, finely chopped

4 small fresh red chillies, finely sliced

110g (4oz) boneless chicken, finely sliced

1 tablespoon fish sauce

1/2 teaspoon sugar

1 tablespoon light soy sauce

450g (1lb) boiled fragrant rice (see page 106)

1 small onion, sliced

2 spring onions, sliced into 2.5cm (1in) lengths

Coriander leaves, to garnish

In a wok or frying pan, heat the oil and fry the garlic until golden brown. Add the chillies and chicken and stir quickly. Add the fish sauce, sugar and light soy sauce, stir and cook for a few seconds until the chicken is cooked through. Add the cooked rice and stir thoroughly. Add the onion and spring onions and stir quickly to mix.

Turn on to a serving dish and garnish with the coriander leaves.

Preparation time: 3 minutes   Cooking time: 5 minutes

fried rice with prawns and green curry paste
khao pad kiow wan gung

2 tablespoons oil

2 garlic cloves, finely chopped

1 tablespoon green curry paste (see page 73)

120g (4oz) raw prawns, peeled and de-veined

2 tablespoons fish sauce

1/4 teaspoon sugar

1 tablespoon light soy sauce

450g (1lb) boiled fragrant rice (see page 106)

1 sweet red pepper, deseeded and sliced

2 spring onions, sliced into 2.5cm (1in) lengths

Coriander leaves, to garnish

In a wok or frying pan, heat the oil until a light haze appears. Add the garlic and fry until golden brown. Add the green curry paste and the prawns and stir quickly. Add the fish sauce, sugar and soy sauce, stir and cook for a few seconds until the prawns are opaque and cooked through. Add the cooked rice and stir thoroughly. Add the sweet pepper and spring onions and stir quickly to mix.

Turn on to a serving dish and garnish with the coriander leaves.

Preparation time: 5 minutes   Cooking time: 5 minutes

fried rice with chicken and curry powder
khao pad karee gai

2 tablespoons oil
2 garlic cloves, finely chopped
1 teaspoon medium-hot curry powder
75g (3oz) boneless chicken, finely sliced
450g (1lb) boiled fragrant rice (see page 106)
1 tablespoon light soy sauce
2 tablespoons fish sauce
1/2 teaspoon sugar
2 spring onions, sliced into 2.5cm (1in) lengths
1/2 small onion, finely sliced
Pinch of ground white pepper

In a wok or frying pan, heat the oil and fry the garlic until golden brown. Add the curry powder, stir and cook for a few seconds. Add the chicken and cook for a minute or two until the meat is opaque. Add the cooked rice and stir thoroughly. Add the light soy sauce, fish sauce and sugar, stirring after each addition. Cook together for a few seconds until you are sure the meat is cooked through and the rice thoroughly reheated.

Turn on to a serving dish, garnish with the spring onions and onion, and lightly sprinkle with pepper.

Preparation time: 3 minutes   Cooking time: 5 minutes

fried rice with pork and chillies
khao pad moo

2 tablespoons oil
2 garlic cloves, finely chopped
110g (4oz) lean pork, finely diced
1 egg
1 tablespoon fish sauce
1 teaspoon sugar
1 tablespoon light soy sauce
450g (1lb) boiled fragrant rice (see page 106)
1 small onion, sliced
1/2 red or green sweet pepper, deseeded and sliced
1/2 teaspoon ground white pepper
1 spring onion, green part only, sliced into 2.5cm (1in) lengths
Coriander leaves, to garnish

In a wok or frying pan, heat the oil until a light haze appears. Add the garlic and fry until golden brown. Add the pork and stir quickly; break the egg into the pan and stir quickly. Add the fish sauce, sugar and light soy sauce, then stir and cook for a few seconds until the pork is cooked through. Add the cooked rice and stir thoroughly. Add the onion, sweet pepper, white pepper and spring onion and stir quickly to mix.

Turn on to a serving dish and garnish with the coriander leaves.

Preparation time: 3 minutes   Cooking time: 5 minutes

beef fried rice with basil leaves
khao pad krapow nua

2 tablespoons oil

2 garlic cloves, finely chopped

3 small fresh red chillies, finely chopped

110g (4oz) minced beef

2 tablespoons fish sauce

½ teaspoon sugar

1 tablespoon light soy sauce

225g (8oz) boiled fragrant rice (see page 106)

1 small onion, sliced

20 holy basil leaves

In a wok or frying pan, heat the oil and fry the garlic until golden brown. Add the chillies and minced beef and stir quickly to mix. Add the fish sauce, sugar and light soy sauce. Stir-fry until the beef is cooked through.

Add the cooked rice and stir thoroughly. Add the onion and basil leaves, stirring quickly. Turn on to a serving dish and serve.

Preparation time: 3 minutes   Cooking time: 5 minutes

sticky rice and pork and chilli sauce
khao niew nam prik ong

2 tablespoons oil

2 garlic cloves, finely chopped

2 teaspoons red curry paste (see page 72)

75g (3oz) minced pork

1 large tomato, finely chopped

2 tablespoons fish sauce

1 tablespoon lemon juice

1 teaspoon sugar

Sticky rice (see page 107), to serve

In a wok or frying pan, heat the oil until a light haze appears. Add the garlic and fry until golden brown. Mix in the curry paste and cook together briefly. Add the pork and stir-fry until the meat loses its pink colour.

Add the tomato, stir and cook for 2–3 seconds, then add the fish sauce, lemon juice and sugar. Stir together for 2 minutes to thoroughly blend the flavours.

Turn the mixture into a small bowl and serve with sticky rice.

Preparation time: 3 minutes   Cooking time: 8 minutes

noodles
gueyteow

Noodles are a Chinese invention, but have become the basic fast food of most of Asia. In Thailand there are noodle sellers everywhere, more or less at any time of the day or night.

Noodles are made from either rice flour or soya bean flour and there are six main varieties.

Sen yai

Sometimes called rice river noodle or rice stick, this is a broad, flat, white rice flour noodle. If bought fresh, the strands need to be separated before cooking.

Sen mee

A small, wiry noodle, sometimes called rice vermicelli.

Sen lek

A medium-sized, flat rice flour noodle. The city of Chantaburi is famous for these noodles, which are sometimes called Jantaboon noodles, after the nickname for the town.

Ba mee

An egg and rice flour noodle, yellow in colour, this comes in a variety of shapes, each with its own name. However, it is unlikely that you will see anything other than the commonest form, which is like a thin spaghetti, curled up in nests, which need to be shaken loose before cooking.

Wun sen

A very thin, wiry, translucent soya bean flour noodle, also called vermicelli or cellophane noodle.

Kanom jin

The one uniquely Thai noodle, made from rice flour mixed with water, then squeezed through a special sieve to make thick strands, like spaghetti. It is made only in large quantities for special occasions, usually temple festivals. Luckily there is a very similar Japanese noodle, *longxu*, which is sold dried in packets, in specialist shops.

Dried noodles

All dried noodles, with the exception of *ba mee* noodles, need to be soaked in cold water for about 20 minutes before cooking (*wun sen* noodles need a little less time). The dry weight will generally double with soaking. After soaking, drain the noodles before cooking. Cooking is generally a matter of dunking them in boiling water for 2 or 3 seconds.

the four flavours
kruang prung

While each noodle dish has its own distinctive taste, the final flavour is left to the diner, who can adjust it by sprinkling on quite small amounts of the four flavours. These are always put out in small bowls, wherever noodles are served. The flavours are:

Chillies in fish sauce *Prik Nam Pla*

4 small fresh red or green chillies, finely chopped, in 4 tablespoons fish sauce.

Chillies in rice vinegar *Prik Nam Som*

4 small fresh red or green chillies, finely chopped, in 4 tablespoons rice vinegar.

Sugar *Nam Tan*

Chilli powder *Prik Pon*

thai fried noodles
gueytoew pad thai

3 tablespoons oil

1 garlic clove, finely chopped

50g (2oz) ready-fried beancurd, cut into 1cm (1/2in) cubes

1 egg

*110g (4oz) dried sen lek noodles, soaked in water for 20 minutes,
drained*

1 tablespoon finely chopped chi po (preserved turnip)

2 spring onions, cut into 2.5cm (1in) pieces

2 tablespoons chopped roasted peanuts

75g (3oz) beansprouts

1/2 teaspoon chilli powder

1 teaspoon sugar

2 tablespoons light soy sauce

1 tablespoon lemon juice

1 sprig of coriander, coarsely chopped

1 lemon wedge

In a wok or frying pan, heat the oil and fry the garlic until golden brown. Add the beancurd and stir. Break the egg into the wok, cook for a moment, then stir. Add the noodles, stir well, then add the chi po and spring onions with half the peanuts and half the beansprouts.

Stir well, then add the chilli powder, sugar, light soy sauce and lemon juice. Stir well and turn on to a plate. Sprinkle with the remaining peanuts and chopped coriander sprig. Arrange the remaining beansprouts and lemon wedge on the side of the plate: these can be added by the diner to their own taste.

Preparation time: 10 minutes   Cooking time: 5 minutes

fried noodles with black fungus mushrooms
mee pad het jay

2 tablespoons oil

50g (2oz) onions, coarsely chopped

*50g (2oz) sen mee noodles (dry weight), soaked in water for
20 minutes and drained*

*50g (2oz) black fungus mushrooms, soaked in water and drained,
then coarsely chopped*

50g (2oz) celery, coarsely chopped

50g (2oz) tomatoes, coarsely chopped

2 tablespoons light soy sauce

1 tablespoon sugar

1/2 teaspoon ground white pepper

Coriander leaves, to garnish

Heat the oil in a wok or large frying pan and fry the onions briefly. Add all the remaining ingredients except the coriander in succession, stirring between each addition.

As soon as the ground pepper is stirred in, turn the mixture on to a plate, garnish with the coriander and serve.

Preparation time: 5 minutes   Cooking time: 3 minutes

egg noodles with stir-fried vegetables
mee sua

2 tablespoons oil
1 garlic clove, finely chopped
1 large dried red chilli, roughly chopped
6 raw king prawns, peeled and de-veined
110g (4oz) ready-cooked egg noodles
1 celery stalk, finely chopped
50g (2oz) beansprouts
2 spring onions, finely chopped
1 medium tomato, cut into segments
1/2 teaspoon chilli powder
2 tablespoons light soy sauce
1 tablespoon fish sauce
1/2 teaspoon sugar

In a wok or frying pan, heat the oil until a light haze appears. Fry the garlic, after a moment add the chilli and continue stir-frying until the garlic is golden. Add the prawns and cook briefly until they start to become opaque.

Add the noodles, stir well, then add all the remaining ingredients, stirring quickly. Turn on to a serving dish.

Preparation time: 10 minutes   Cooking time: 3 minutes

deep-fried noodles with mixed vegetables
mee krop lad nah

1 nest of egg noodles
Oil for deep-frying

For the mixed vegetables
2 tablespoons oil
1 garlic clove, finely chopped
50g (2oz) bamboo shoots, finely sliced
50g (2oz) straw mushrooms
4 baby sweetcorn, cut in half lengthways
1 small sweet red or green pepper, deseeded and diced
2 spring onions, chopped into 2.5cm (1in) lengths
2 tablespoons light soy sauce
1 teaspoon dark soy sauce
1 teaspoon sugar
1/2 teaspoon ground white pepper
1 tablespoon cornflour, mixed with 125ml (4fl oz) vegetable stock or water to make a thin paste
Coriander leaves, to garnish

Separate the strands of egg noodle. Heat the oil and deep-fry the noodles until crisp. Remove from the oil and drain. Place the noodles on a serving dish and set aside.

Heat the oil in a wok or frying pan until a light haze appears. Fry the garlic until golden brown. Add the remaining ingredients, except for the cornflour paste and coriander, stirring constantly. Finally stir in the flour paste. Pour over the noodles, garnish with the coriander and serve.

Preparation time: 5 minutes   Cooking time: 8 minutes

fried noodles with crab
mee pad pod

2 tablespoons oil

1 garlic clove, finely chopped

1 teaspoon red curry paste (see page 72)

120g (4oz) crab meat

1 egg, lightly beaten

110g (4oz) sen mee noodles (dry weight), soaked in water for
   20 minutes and drained

50g (2oz) beansprouts

3 spring onions, thinly sliced

1 tablespoon fish sauce

1 tablespoon light soy sauce

1 teaspoon sugar

1 large fresh red chilli, finely chopped

2 tablespoons lime juice

Heat the oil in a wok or frying pan and fry the garlic until golden
brown. Add the remaining ingredients in succession, stirring well
between each addition. Cook for a further minute or two, turn on to
a plate and serve.

Preparation time: 3 minutes   Cooking time: 5 minutes

egg noodles with squid
ba mee plamuk

1 nest of dried ba mee egg noodles

175g (6oz) squid, cleaned and roughly chopped

110g (4oz) white cabbage, roughly chopped

1 tablespoon fish sauce

1 tablespoon light soy sauce

1 teaspoon sugar

2 tablespoons lime juice

2 small fresh red chillies, finely chopped

2 spring onions, finely chopped

2 tablespoons ground roasted peanuts

Bring a pan of water to the boil, add the noodles and simmer until
they soften and separate. Remove, drain and hold under cold
running water to stop the cooking process. Drain well again and
set aside.

Place the squid in a pan, cover with water and bring to the boil.
Remove, drain and set aside. Dip the white cabbage quickly into the
boiling water, drain and set aside.

Place the noodles, squid, white cabbage and all the remaining
ingredients in a bowl and mix well. Turn on to a plate and serve.

Preparation time: 5 minutes   Cooking time: 5 minutes

spicy pork noodles with lime leaves

pad ki mow

1 tablespoon oil

1 garlic clove, finely chopped

1–2 small fresh red or green chillies, finely chopped

110g (4oz) lean pork, thinly sliced

1 tablespoon fish sauce

1 tablespoon dark soy sauce

1 teaspoon sugar

2 Kaffir lime leaves, finely chopped

1 medium tomato, chopped

110g (4oz) soaked sen yai noodles (dry weight), rinsed and separated

1 sprig of coriander, coarsely chopped, to garnish

In a wok or frying pan, heat the oil and fry the garlic until golden brown. Add the chillies and stir for a couple of seconds, then add the pork and stir well. In succession add the fish sauce, dark soy sauce, sugar and Kaffir lime leaves, stirring quickly after each addition.

Add the tomato, stir until cooked and then add the noodles. Stir briefly until cooked through. Turn on to a serving dish and garnish with the coriander.

Preparation time: 5 minutes   Cooking time: 5 minutes

egg noodles with seafood

ba mee talay

1 nest of fresh or dried ba mee noodles

2 tablespoons oil

2 garlic cloves, finely chopped

50g (2oz) raw prawns, peeled and de-veined

50g (2oz) crab meat

50g (2oz) fresh or tinned bamboo shoots, sliced

8–10 fresh or tinned straw mushrooms, halved

1 tablespoon light soy sauce

1 tablespoon dark soy sauce

2 tablespoons fish sauce

Pinch of sugar

4 tablespoons vegetable stock

Ground white pepper

1 tablespoon flour, mixed with 2 tablespoons water

1 spring onion, coarsely chopped

If using fresh noodles, shake the strands loose and set aside. Bring a saucepan of water to the boil. Using a coarse-meshed strainer or a sieve, dip the noodles (either fresh or dried) into the boiling water. If fresh, leave only for a few seconds; if dry, leave until the nest separates into strands, at which point the noodles should be soft. Drain and set aside.

In a wok or frying pan, heat half the oil and fry half the garlic until golden brown. Add the noodles and stir-fry briefly until darker and no longer wet. Turn on to a serving dish and keep hot.

Quickly heat the remaining oil in the pan and fry the remaining garlic until golden brown. Add the seafood and stir until cooked through. Add the bamboo shoots and straw mushrooms and stir. Add the light and dark soy sauces, the fish sauce, sugar, stock and a sprinkling of pepper, stirring briefly after each new addition. Add enough of the flour and water mixture to thicken the sauce slightly and cook for 1–2 minutes. Add the spring onion, stir and turn on to the noodles. Serve.

Preparation time: 5 minutes **Cooking time: 7 minutes**

grilled pork with rice noodles

sen mee moo yang

450g (1lb) pork loin, sliced across the grain into very thin strips

150g (5oz) rice noodles (dry weight)

120g (4oz) beansprouts

110g (4oz) carrots, chopped into fine matchsticks

110g (4oz) white radish (mooli), chopped into fine matchsticks

110g (4oz) cucumber, chopped into fine matchsticks

30 basil leaves

For the marinade

1 large garlic clove, finely chopped

1 young lemon grass stalk, finely chopped

1 teaspoon five-spice powder

2 tablespoons fish sauce

1 teaspoon sugar

1 teaspoon sesame oil

For the dressing

1 teaspoon sugar

5 tablespoons hot water

2 tablespoons fish sauce

2 tablespoons vinegar

1 garlic clove, finely chopped

2 small fresh red chillies, finely chopped

In a bowl, mix together the marinade ingredients, stirring well. Add the pork strips, toss to coat thoroughly and leave to marinate for 30 minutes.

Bring a large pan of water to the boil. Dip the rice noodles in the water for 1 minute. Remove and hold under cold running water to stop the cooking process. Drain again and leave to cool.

To make the dressing, dissolve the sugar in the hot water and add all the remaining ingredients. Stir well and set aside.

Arrange the rice noodles and all the vegetables and basil leaves in a bowl and set aside.

Preheat a barbecue or grill until it is very hot. Cook the pork slices for 3 seconds only on each side, then place on a warmed serving dish.

Pour the dressing over the noodles, toss well and serve with the pork.

Marinating time: 30 minutes   Cooking time: 5 minutes

minced pork noodles with curry powder
gueyteow moo sap

Lettuce leaves

2 tablespoons oil

*110g (4oz) sen yai noodles (dry weight), rinsed for 20 minutes
  and separated*

1 tablespoon dark soy sauce

1 garlic clove, finely chopped

110g (4oz) minced lean pork

1 tablespoon tang chi (preserved radish)

125ml (4fl oz) stock (have more to hand)

1 teaspoon curry powder

1 small onion, finely sliced

1 tablespoon fish sauce

1 tablespoon plain flour, mixed with a little water to form a thin paste

2 small spring onions, finely chopped

Line a serving dish with roughly torn lettuce.

Heat half the oil in a wok or frying pan. Add the noodles, stir quickly and add $1/2$ teaspoon of the dark soy sauce. Stir for 30–60 seconds to prevent sticking. Turn on to the prepared serving dish.

Heat the remaining oil and fry the garlic until golden brown, add the pork and stir quickly until the meat is lightly cooked. Add the rest of the ingredients in turn, including the remaining soy sauce, stirring briefly after each addition. The flour and water paste will thicken the sauce; add only 1 teaspoon at a time. Add more stock if the mixture becomes too dry. Turn the pork mixture on to the noodles and serve.

Preparation time: 5 minutes   Cooking time: 5 minutes

spicy noodles with pork and prawns
guey teow yum

4 lettuce leaves

110g (4oz) sen yai noodles (dry weight), rinsed and separated

75g (3oz) pork, finely sliced

75g (3oz) raw prawns, peeled and de-veined

1 garlic clove, finely chopped

2 small fresh red chillies, finely chopped

1 tablespoon fish sauce

1 tablespoon lime juice

1 teaspoon sugar

75g (3oz) celery, finely sliced

1 tablespoon ground roasted peanuts

Arrange the lettuce leaves on a serving dish and set aside.

In a saucepan of boiling water, blanch the noodles for 2–3 seconds. Strain (reserving the water) and turn into a bowl. Cook the pork and prawns in the reserved water until both are cooked, then turn into the bowl.

Add all the remaining ingredients to the bowl, stirring well. Turn on to the lettuce-lined serving dish.

Preparation time: 5 minutes   Cooking time: 5 minutes

beef curry noodles

gueyteow kaek

50g (2oz) sen lek noodles (dry weight), soaked in cold water for
  15 minutes and drained
110g (4oz) beef, cut into small cubes
1 hard-boiled egg
3 tablespoons oil
50g (2oz) ready-fried beancurd, finely sliced
1 shallot, finely sliced
1 garlic clove, finely chopped
2 teaspoons red curry paste (see page 72)
4 tablespoons coconut milk
1 teaspoon curry powder
2 tablespoons fish sauce
1 teaspoon sugar
1 tablespoon ground roasted peanuts
Coriander leaves, to garnish

Set the noodles aside, but have ready a pan of hot water in which to warm them. Put the beef in a small pan and cover with water; boil gently for 5–10 minutes. Shell the egg, cut into quarters and set aside.

Heat 1 tablespoon of oil and fry the sliced beancurd until slightly crisp; drain and set aside. Reheat the oil (add a little more if necessary) and fry the shallot until dark golden brown and crisp. Set aside in the pan.

In a separate wok or frying pan, heat the remaining oil, add the garlic and fry for a few seconds until golden brown. Add the curry paste, stir to mix and cook for a few seconds. Add the coconut milk, stir thoroughly to blend and heat through for a few seconds.

With a slotted spoon or strainer, remove the beef from its pan (reserve the cooking water) and add to the mixture in the wok. Stir to make sure each piece of meat is covered with the curry. Add 2 cups of the water in which the beef has boiled (make up the amount with cold water if necessary), the curry powder, fish sauce and sugar. Stir to mix and cook together for about 5 minutes.

Have two serving bowls ready. Bring the pan of hot water for the noodles to the boil, put the noodles in a sieve or strainer with a handle and dip into the water for 2–3 seconds to warm through. Drain and divide between the serving bowls. Arrange the quartered egg on top of the noodles. Add the peanuts to the beef curry, stir and pour over the noodles. Garnish with the reserved fried beancurd, the fried shallots with a little of their oil, and the coriander.

Preparation time: 10 minutes   Cooking time: 10 minutes

spicy pork and vermicelli noodle soup
wun sen tom yum

1 tablespoon oil

1 garlic clove, finely chopped

300ml (1/2 pint) chicken stock

1 teaspoon tang chi (preserved radish)

110g (4oz) pork, finely sliced

75g (3oz) wun sen noodles (dry weight), soaked for 20 minutes
  and drained

25g (1oz) beansprouts

2 tablespoons fish sauce

1 teaspoon sugar

1 tablespoon lime juice

1/2 teaspoon chilli powder

2 teaspoons ground roasted peanuts

1 spring onion, finely chopped

In a small pan, heat the oil and fry the garlic until golden brown.
Remove from the heat and set aside.

In a saucepan, heat the stock and tang chi. When it is simmering, add
the pork slices and all the other ingredients except the garlic oil. When
the soup comes to the boil, it is ready to serve: ladle into soup bowls
and sprinkle a little of the garlic oil on top.

Preparation time: 3 minutes   Cooking time: 5 minutes

chicken noodles with basil leaves
lahd nah

2 tablespoons oil

110g (4oz) sen mee noodles (dry weight), soaked in water for
  20 minutes and drained

2 tablespoons light soy sauce

2 garlic cloves, finely chopped

2 fresh red chillies, finely sliced

110g (4oz) boneless chicken, finely sliced

20 basil leaves

1 tablespoon fish sauce

4 tablespoons stock or water (have more to hand)

1 teaspoon plain flour, mixed with 3 tablespoons water to a
  thin paste

50g (2oz) mangetout

50g (2oz) carrots, sliced into matchsticks

1 teaspoon sugar

In a wok or frying pan, heat 1 tablespoon of the oil. Add the noodles
and stir quickly, then add 1 tablespoon of the light soy sauce and stir
well for 30–60 seconds, to prevent sticking. Turn on to a serving dish.

Add the remaining oil to the wok, heat, then fry the garlic and chillies
until golden brown. Add the chicken, stir and cook briefly, then add
the basil leaves, fish sauce and the remaining soy sauce and stir. Add a
little stock or water and stir. Add the flour and water mixture and stir
in thoroughly. Stir in the vegetables and sugar. Cook for a few seconds
until the chicken is cooked through, stirring constantly. Add a little
more stock if necessary. Stir, then turn on to the noodles and serve.

Preparation time: 5 minutes   Cooking time: 8 minutes

fried chicken noodles with curry paste
ba mee pad prik gaeng

2 tablespoons oil

2 small garlic cloves, finely chopped

1 tablespoon red curry paste (see page 72)

175g (6oz) boneless chicken, roughly chopped

75g (3oz) or 1 nest of egg noodles, soaked if dried

1 tablespoon dark soy sauce

1 tablespoon light soy sauce

1 teaspoon sugar

50g (2oz) beansprouts

50g (2oz) broccoli, cut into small florets

50g (2oz) carrots, cut into fine matchsticks

Coriander leaves, to garnish

In a wok or large frying pan, heat the oil and fry the garlic until golden brown. Add the curry paste and stir well. Next, add all the remaining ingredients in succession except the coriander, stirring once between each addition.

Mix well, turn out on to a serving dish and garnish with the coriander leaves.

Preparation time: 3 minutes   Cooking time: 5 minutes

stir-fried noodles with
beef and dried chilli
gueyteow pad nua

2 tablespoons oil

2 garlic cloves, finely chopped

1 teaspoon finely chopped fresh ginger

1 large dried red chilli, coarsely chopped

225g (8oz) lean beef, thinly sliced

1 egg

1 medium onion, finely chopped

1 tablespoon fish sauce

1 tablespoon light soy sauce

1 teaspoon sugar

110g (4oz) dried medium flat white flour noodles (dry weight), soaked for 20–30 minutes and drained

110g (4oz) celery, coarsely chopped

Heat the oil in wok or frying pan and fry the garlic until golden brown. Add the ginger and stir, add the chilli and stir, then add the beef and stir until it is just cooked through.

Break the egg into the mixture and stir quickly. Add the onion and stir. Add the fish sauce, light soy sauce and sugar, stir once, then add the noodles and stir well for 1 minute. Add the celery, stir briefly, turn on to a plate and serve.

Preparation time: 5 minutes   Cooking time: 5 minutes

fruits, desserts
& drinks

festivals

Festivals are an essential part of Thai life. For Thai people, the primary purpose of celebrating festivals is to have fun, but they also maintain an important link with the traditions and culture of the past. This is especially true in the rural areas where the year is still dictated by the agricultural cycle, so times of toil are punctuated by seasonal festivals that serve as both holidays and propitious occasions. Many festivals follow the lunar calendar and are thus literally moveable feasts, while others have set annual dates. However, Thai people certainly have many festivals to celebrate throughout the year, whether religious or secular, royal or political.

Perhaps the most important, best-known and greatest of Thailand's festivals is *Songkran*. *Songkran* is the celebration of the traditional Thai New Year, which starts on 13 April and lasts for three days. *Songkran* is a Thai word which means 'move' or 'change place', as it is the day when the sun changes its position in the Zodiac. It is also known as the 'Water Festival' as people believe that water will wash away bad luck. The tradition of *Songkran* is respected by all Thai people irrespective of their status or religion. It is also a family get-together, where the younger members pay respects to their elders by pouring scented water onto the hands of their parents and grandparents, and present them with gifts. They dedicate the merits of this action to their ancestors, and in turn, the elders wish the youngsters good luck and prosperity.

Another popular festival is *Loy Krathong* which is celebrated annually on the full moon day of the 12th lunar month (November). It takes place at a time when the weather is fine, the rainy season is over and there is a high water level all over the country. On this night, everybody goes to rivers and other waterways to float a *krathong*. Traditionally a *krathong* is bowl-shaped and made out of banana leaves, with a lotus flower placed in the middle with a lighted candle in its centre. The purpose of floating the *krathong* is firstly to pay homage to the Lord Buddha and the spirits of the water on which the agricultural society depends for its prosperity, and secondly for releasing trouble and bad luck, which is symbolically carried away on the water.

The Fruit Fair (right and previous pages) is an annual event, usually held during the middle of May, celebrating the abundance of local fruits and products. As well as the stalls that sell local fruits and products, there are colourful floats decorated with fruits, parades and musical and dance processions, beauty pageants, fruit competitions and exhibitions of local produce.

thai fruits, desserts and drinks kong-wan, kanom, krueng-deum

Thai desserts and sweets are almost a separate cuisine in themselves. As much care, skill and artistry goes into their creation as that applied in the best European patisseries. In Thailand fresh fruit is the normal finale to a meal; sweet desserts are reserved for special occasions and formal entertaining, mainly because they need a lot of preparation and cooking time. Consequently I have not included recipes for them here but have concentrated on Thai fruits, desserts and drinks that can be prepared quickly and easily.

Thailand is popularly known as the 'land of smiles' though it should be just as well known as a country blessed with a myriad of delicious tropical and temperate fruits. It is a paradise for those who love fruit. Generally Thai fruits are sweet, but there are some that are sour, like tamarind. The major fruit-producing areas are located mostly in the eastern and southern regions of the country, but the central region also produces a variety of fruit for the markets in every season.

Thailand is never without fruit. In the countryside, some fruit trees, such as banana trees, double as fences around people's houses. Though they make a much less impenetrable barrier than barbed wire, they provide greenery and fresh air to all living nearby.

durian
du-rian

The durian, king of fruits, is Thailand's most expensive fruit. It looks like a rugby ball, ranges from 15 to 25cm (6 to 10in) long and can weigh up to 4.5kg (10lb). The rind is covered with very sharp spines and the fruit is therefore carried by the stem or on an attached string to avoid damage to the hands. Durian is a distinctive and unusual-tasting fruit. Inside are five sections with from one to several seeds encased within a cream or yellow aromatic, custard-like pulp. The flavour is intriguing and difficult to describe – a custard with almonds, onion and cream cheese might give some idea of this wonderful fruit. People either love it or hate it. It has a very strong aroma, so strong in fact that it is banned from airline cabins, hotels and some public transport.

Durian is referred to as a 'heating' fruit that causes the body to feel warm. Over-consumption is said to be balanced by eating a 'cooling' fruit like the mangosteen. A commonly held belief is that drinking alcoholic beverages after eating durian can cause illness or death. I have seen many test this belief, but no one succumbed!

durian with coconut sweet sticky rice
nam grati durian

225ml (8fl oz) coconut milk
1/2 teaspoon salt
75g (3oz) sugar
1 ripe durian, peeled, stoned and cut into pieces

For the coconut sweet sticky rice
125ml (4fl oz) coconut milk
1/2 teaspoon salt
50g (2oz) sugar
225g (8oz) freshly cooked sticky rice (see page 107)

To make the coconut sweet sticky rice, mix the coconut milk, salt and sugar in a bowl until the sugar has dissolved. Stir in the still-warm sticky rice and set aside.

To prepare the fruit mixture, heat the coconut milk with the salt and sugar until the sugar dissolves. Remove from the heat and allow to cool. Place the durian pieces in the cooled mixture and leave to soak briefly.

Arrange the durian on a serving dish beside the sweet sticky rice and serve.

Preparation time: 5 minutes   Cooking time: 30 minutes

mangosteen
mang-kut

The mangosteen is my all-time favourite fruit. Not well known outside Thailand, it is about 5cm (2in) in diameter and has a thick purple/black, woody skin. Inside are segments (similar to those in an orange) of sweet, juicy white flesh. The taste is very refreshing, being both sweet and tart, and the pulp melts on to your tongue. Everyone likes the mangosteen the first time they try it, and many feel it is the finest fruit in the world. Unfortunately it is very hard to grow, and also bruises very easily while being transported, the consequent wastage tending to make it expensive.

mango
ma-muang

One of the great fruits of Thailand with a special reputation all its own, the mango comes in several different varieties, used in different ways. It can be eaten unripe, almost white, when it is very crunchy and sour. This is a great favourite in Thailand: it is sliced and eaten with chilli dips, a combination which caters perfectly to the Thai love of crunchy texture with sharp, sour tastes. Dessert mangoes have a juicy, orange flesh and can be sliced and eaten on their own, another great favourite. Many feel the best way to enjoy mango is with sticky rice and coconut milk – a popular Thai dessert. Mangoes can also be used for making ice cream and sorbet.

mango sorbet
ma-muang sobey

450g (1lb) ripe mango, peeled, stoned and chopped
150g (5oz) sugar, dissolved in 1 cupful of water to make a syrup

Blend the mango with the cooled syrup until the mixture is smooth. Put it into the freezer in a suitable container for about 1 hour until the mixture is slushy and frozen round the edges. Remove and reblend, then return to the freezer for about 30 minutes.

Serve the sorbet with fresh fruit.

Preparation time: 15 minutes   Freezing time: 1 hour 30 minutes

papaya
ma-la-kaw

The delicious papaya is available most of the year, but is at its best during the hot season, from March to July. Oval in shape, the fruit is cut lengthways to remove the small black seeds in the middle. As with the mango, the papaya is used both unripe and ripe. The best-known use, when the fruit is a very pale beige, is in *Som Tam* (see page 46), for which it is grated, but it can also be used as a vegetable and cooked, generally in curries. When the fruit is ripe, the soft, dark-orange coloured flesh is full of flavour, and can be eaten raw with a sprinkling of lime juice to contrast with its sweetness. Combining papaya in a fruit salad with pineapple or melon such as cantaloupe, is delectable.

banana
kluay

European people are generally familiar only with one type of banana imported there. In Thailand we have many different sorts, growing in abundance. Not only the fruit is used; the leaves make an excellent platter, plate decoration or wrapper for all kinds of food. Thai bananas range in size from the smallest lady's finger upwards, the tastes and textures also varying widely. The most famous type is *Kluay Hom,* a large specimen with a thick golden skin. Unripe bananas are sliced and dried in the sun, fried or grilled for a snack. Ripe bananas are sweet and fragrant and nice for eating fresh. Unripe bananas are also preserved in sugar or used in baking. Popular Thai banana dishes are *Kluay Ping* (grilled and soaked with syrup), *Kluay Buat Chi* (boiled in coconut milk), *Kluay Chiuam* (boiled in syrup), *Kluay Phao* (smoked in the skin) and *Kluay Khaek* (golden fritters). Bananas also form the basis for a good milk shake, and can be dipped in batter (made with rice flour and coconut milk) and deep-fried.

bananas cooked in syrup
kluay chuíam

225g (8oz) sugar
225ml (8fl oz) water
4 large bananas
125ml (4fl oz) coconut milk, mixed with 1/4 teaspoon salt, to serve
  (optional)

In a small saucepan, dissolve the sugar in the water. Strain through muslin into a large pan. Peel the bananas and chop into 5cm (2in) pieces. Add to the sugar mixture and bring to the boil. Reduce the heat and cook gently, removing any scum that forms, until the bananas are bright and clear and the sugar syrup forms threads when lifted with a wooden spoon. Serve hot as it is, or with the coconut milk mixed with salt to balance the sweetness.

Preparation time: 3 minutes   **Cooking time: 30 minutes**

coconut
ma-prow

The coconut palm is one of the most versatile of trees, the fruit used in many ways, the leaves for roofs and screens, the sap to make coconut sugar, and the wood itself to make houses. The young coconut, with either a green or yellow exterior, is full of water (not milk), which is sweet, refreshing and very healthy, a perfect drink. No matter where a coconut grows, the water inside the nut is pure and safe. Vendors selling drinking nuts will open them for you and even give you a straw. After the water has been consumed, the shell is broken open and the immature, jelly-like flesh is scraped out with a spoon and eaten. Alternatively the pulp may be mixed with water, then squeezed to make coconut milk, used in many dishes. The flesh of the mature coconut is grated and used in cakes and desserts including ice cream.

coconut ice cream
ice cream grati

225ml (8fl oz) coconut milk
175ml (6fl oz) whipping cream
60g (2¹/₂oz) sugar
3 tablespoons finely chopped young coconut flesh, or 2 tablespoons
* unsweetened desiccated coconut, toasted*
2 eggs

In a saucepan, combine the coconut milk, whipping cream, sugar and coconut flesh or desiccated coconut in saucepan and bring to the boil. Beat the eggs in a bowl, then whisk the boiling coconut milk mixture into the egg. Allow to cool.

Pour the mixture into a small loaf tin, cover and freeze until firm. Break up the ice cream, then beat in a bowl with an electric mixer or in a food-processor until smooth. Spoon the mixture back into the tin, cover and freeze for several hours until firm.

Preparation time: 10 minutes   Freezing time: 3 hours

pumpkin in coconut milk
gaeng buad fak tong

225ml (8fl oz) coconut milk
225g (8oz) pumpkin, peeled and cut into 2.5cm (1in) cubes
4 tablespoons sugar

In a pan, bring the coconut milk to the boil and add the pumpkin and sugar, and simmer until the pumpkin is soft. When ready, turn onto a serving dish.

Preparation time: 5 minutes   Cooking time: 5 minutes

rambutan
ngoh

The name of this fruit is derived from the Malay word *rambut* meaning hair. This is because the fruit's rind is covered with red and yellow spikes. Thai rambutans, grown mostly in the south and east, are sweet and succulent, the juicy flesh coming easily away from the stone. Favourite varieties are *Ngoh Rong Rien* and *Ngoh Si Chompoo*. Thais are experts at delicately carving away the sweet flesh from the central stone.

rambutan in syrup
ngoh loy geow

225g (8oz) sugar
450ml (16fl oz) water
8 rambutans, peeled and stoned
Crushed ice, to serve

In a small saucepan, bring the sugar and water gently to the boil, stirring occasionally. Boil for 10 minutes, until a thin syrup has formed. Put the rambutans in a bowl, pour the syrup over them and stir well. Serve with ice to make them really cold.

Preparation time: 5 minutes   Cooking time: 12 minutes

longan
lam-yai

The longan is one of north Thailand's most succulent fruit. You will see longans, or 'dragon's eyes', in Chiangmai's markets and supermarkets – clusters of small, brown fruit (about the size of a large grape), still attached to a bouquet of thin branches and green leaves. This is the best way to eat them, straight from the branch as nature intended. The outer 'shell' is very thin and readily peeled away to reveal the moist, juicy interior. The flesh, not unlike that of a lychee, surrounds a shiny, brown seed and is opalescent with a delicate flavour, giving a good balance between sweetness and acidity.

The Thai longan is known as one of the best in the world, the sweet, pinkish-white flesh believed by many to energise the body and banish fatigue. Longans can be enjoyed as a dessert either with sugar syrup or with sticky rice.

sago and longan in coconut milk
lamyai saku peeak

600ml (1 pint) water
50g (2oz) sago
225g (8oz) sugar
110g (4oz) longans, stoned
125ml (4fl oz) coconut milk, mixed with 1/2 teaspoon salt, to serve

In a large pan, bring the water to the boil, add the sago and cook until it swells. Add the sugar and longans, and cook briefly.

Turn into serving bowls and cover with the coconut milk and salt mixture to taste.

Preparation time: 5 minutes   **Cooking time: 5 minutes**

guava
farang

The guava is a well-known fruit that is plentiful in Thailand, though it originated in Spain. Thai people call it by the same name as that used for Westerners (*farang*). A great snack, it is eaten either ripe or when still green, dipped in a little salt or sugar. Guavas also taste great when conserved and are the basis of luscious, highly refreshing drinks. There are many kinds of guava; when peeled, they reveal white, bright red or pink flesh. The white-fleshed is widely available in Thailand, and is the most popular.

pomelo
som-o

A member of the citrus family, the pomelo is similar to a grapefruit, although its sections can be peeled apart more easily. The flesh is succulent, with a delicious sour-sweet flavour. The finest Thai pomelos are those from the central region, especially from Nakhon Pathom, Chai Nat and Phichit. Sweet and tangy, pomelos can be enjoyed in a salad or on their own with sugar syrup.

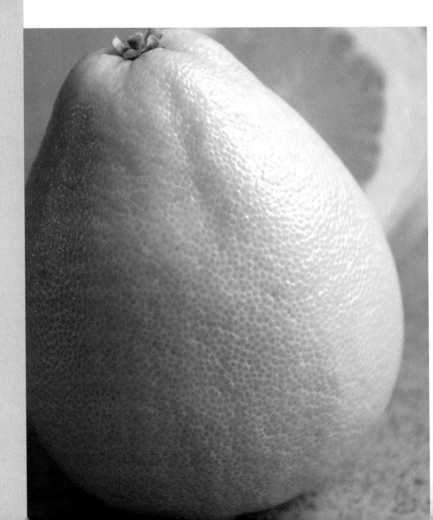

pineapple
sapparot

Thailand is one of the largest producers of this flavourful, juicy fruit, which is best grown in sandy coastal soil. The pineapple grows year-round, not on a tree as might be expected, but on a low plant. Pineapple is a versatile fruit that can be used for desserts, drinks and savoury dishes.

pineapple conserve
sapparot guan

In Thailand we use brass pans for cooking fruit with sugar, but you could use one made from good-quality stainless steel. This conserve will keep for one month, and is delicious served with ice cream.

240g (8oz) sugar
1 pineapple, weighing about 1kg (2¼lb), peeled, cored, finely chopped

In a saucepan, dissolve the sugar in 1 cupful of water over a gentle heat and add the pineapple. Mix thoroughly and stir over a medium heat until the mixture reaches the 'soft ball' stage, then allow to cool.

Preparation time: 10 minutes   Cooking time: 30 minutes

rose apple
chom-poo

Similar in shape to a pear, the rose apple has a glossy skin that is either green or pink in colour. It has a crisp, crunchy texture and an extremely refreshing taste. Thais like to eat it dipped in salt, sugar and chillies.

thai fruit salad
frut sa-lad

4 rose apples, halved, stoned and cut into small cubes

1 ripe mango, peeled, stoned and cut into small cubes

1 small ripe papaya, peeled, deseeded and cut into small cubes

$^{1}/_{2}$ pomelo, peeled, de-rinded, the segments broken apart and cut again into small pieces

$^{1}/_{2}$ pineapple, peeled, cored and cubed

1 tablespoon finely chopped fresh ginger

1 tablespoon lemon juice

1 tablespoon sugar

10 mint leaves, finely chopped

Arrange the fruit in a bowl. Add the ginger, lemon juice, sugar and chopped mint leaves. Mix well and chill in the fridge before serving.

Preparation time: 10 minutes   Cooking time: 0 minutes

watermelon
taeng-mo

The most common watermelon in Thailand is pink-fleshed. The melon is simply cut and sliced lengthways and served plain. The taste is mild but sweet and refreshing. It makes a fabulous drink when blended with ice. The seeds are toasted and eaten as a snack.

watermelon quench
nam taeng-mo pun

2 tablespoons sugar
4 tablespoons water
1 ripe watermelon, peeled
Pinch of salt

In a small pan, gently heat the sugar and water until the sugar dissolves. Allow to cool.

Cut the watermelon into small pieces, removing the seeds and rind. Put some of the pieces into a blender with some ice cubes, the sugar syrup and a pinch of salt to taste. Blend, pour into glasses and serve.

Preparation time: 5 minutes   Cooking time: 0 minutes

tropical fruit drinks
nam-pun

There are many different types of fruit juices enjoyed in Thailand and they are all great thirst-quenchers, especially during the hot months between March and July. A great variety of fruits is used in drinks, including bananas, guavas, papayas, oranges, pineapples, watermelons, coconuts, longans and mangoes.

tea
nam cha

Cha Ron *Hot Tea*
Cha Yen *Iced Tea with Milk*
Cha Dam Yen *Iced Tea without Milk*

In Thailand, tea is grown in the north in hilly areas where the climate is cooler. Sometimes we enjoy our tea hot in the traditional Chinese manner. For iced tea with milk, we make the tea stronger, add sugar and sweetened condensed milk and serve it in a glass with plenty of ice. For iced tea without milk, we add more sugar, stir well, let it cool to room temperature, then pour it over a full glass of ice and garnish with lime slices.

lemon grass tea
nam takrai

1.2 litres (2 pints) water
2 lemon grass stalks, rinsed and lightly crushed, or 50g (2oz) ginger,
  cut into 2.5cm (1in) pieces and roughly sliced
Sugar, to taste

In a saucepan, heat the water. When it begins to boil, add the crushed lemon grass or ginger, cover and continue to boil for 5 minutes.

Pour the contents of the pan into a teapot. Add sugar to taste and serve as hot tea.

coffee
ka fee

I love to have iced coffee with my lunch and as an afternoon drink. In Thailand, we prepare our coffee with condensed milk or sugar syrup instead of fresh milk.

Ka Fee Yen *Iced Coffee with Milk*
Make some strong black coffee, add sugar and sweetened condensed milk and stir well, allow to cool to room temperature, then pour over a full glass of ice and top with unsweetened condensed milk.

Oliang *Sweetened Iced Black Coffee*
Make a strong brew of black coffee. Fill a glass with ice shavings and add the coffee, sweetening to taste with a simple sugar syrup.

Ka Fee Dam *Black Coffee*
A cup of good, strong filtered or percolated coffee.

Ka Fee Ron *Hot Coffee with Milk*
As this coffee is served without sugar, we use tinned, unsweetened evaporated milk.

Ka Fee Dam Ron *Black Coffee with Sugar*
Sugar syrup is added to strong black coffee.

index